IMPORTANT NOTICE

This report is designed to help fill the serious gap in investment literature, covering substantial, timely information on financial privacy and the mechanics and the legal implications of moving assets offshore. These issues can quickly become complicated and emotional. There is an ever expanding body of laws and regulations impacting offshore diversification. Furthermore, for many people, certain privacy initiatives and expatriation of assets raise profound moral dilemmas, such as the decision as to whether the long-term well-being and financial security of oneself and one's family should be superceded by government mandate, for whatever purpose.

Perhaps this report's most vital message is that even the average investor can do a considerable amount to improve his or her financial privacy, without breaking any laws, by acting immediately and hedging against any possible forthcoming government restrictions on foreign travel or investment. Readers must keep in mind that, even though certain offshore diversification strategies may be legal, their administrative complexity may create disadvantages that far outweigh the purported benefits. Final choices are best made in consultation with knowledgeable (and responsible) attorneys, accountants, consultants, and representatives of established offshore financial institutions.

Like so many other important considerations, privacy literally begins at home. Therefore, it is essential to never forget that even the most well-designed privacy programs can be undermined by simply discussing one's activities with persons who need not be privy to such information, including close friends.

Any citations of institutions, persons, publication, strategies, or any other information in this report is for educational purposes only and does not in any way constitute an endorsement or recommendation by The Wealth Institute, the Research Fellows or anyone else associated with the publication and distribution of this report.

ABOUT THE RESEARCH FELLOWS

Mark Skousen

Mark Skousen is the editor of his own monthly newsletter, *Mark Skousen's Forecasts & Strategies*, and is also a consulting editor of *Personal Finance and Tax Angles*. Dr. Skousen has a PhD. in economics from George Washington University and is the author of the best-selling books, *Playing the Price Controls Game*, *The Insider's Banking & Credit Almanac*, *New Profits from Insurance*, *Mark Skousen's Complete Guide to Financial Privacy*, and *High Finance on a Low Budget*.

Skousen has lectured on financial privacy around the world and many of his writings on the topic are considered classics.

Christopher Weber

Christopher Weber is a professional financial researcher and journalist who is highly regarded for his work on the practical assessment of tax havens, precious metals storage, and privacy. Weber was formerly editor and publisher of *Investment Insights*, a newsletter which dealt frequently with these topics. Mr. Weber also consults with offshore financial institutions and assists them in developing programs to suit the needs of Western Hemisphere investors. His major works include: *An Investor's Guide to Tax and Bank Secrecy Havens*, and *How to Buy Precious Metals at Home and Abroad*.

THE CLOSING DOOR: THE END OF FINANCIAL PRIVACY IN AMERICA AND HOW TO PROTECT YOURSELF

TABLE OF CONTENTS

INTRODUCTION

There are two arguments never used when Congress debates policy: the constitutional and the moral. The issue of financial privacy is intimately related to both.

Like so many other issues, the case for financial privacy depends at its very core on a sound understanding of individual rights and the limits of government. With reference to these ideas, most legislators think the case for privacy sounds irrelevant and abstract. And because they refuse to discuss the fundamental philosophy of government, they take the pragmatic route. They deliver obvious blows to freedom and justify them by pointing to the urgent need for seeing the immediate results of a particular policy goal.

Thus privacy has few friends in government. "Liberals" show a respect for civil liberties and often champion the cause of individuals fighting against government intrusion into personal affairs. Witness the accusation repeatedly heard from liberals that conservatives have no respect for the "privacy of the bedroom." But the liberals show little respect for private property rights and are usually willing to use the state's coercive machinery against citizen's property to redistributive ends.

The liberals, then, are utterly inconsistent. They fail to realize that privacy and forced egalitarianism are incompatible ideals. If it is affirmed that the state has the right to total control of an individual's property, to take it by force and to use it according to its own discretion, the state will then attempt to acquire total knowledge about that property even before it is forcefully taken. We are witnessing this phenomenon today.

To counter this "liberal" position, there needs to be a reassertion of the right of the individual to have total ownership of justly acquired property. Once this is established, it necessarily follows that the state has no right to total knowledge about that property. And because the term "privacy" presupposes a definition and clarification of the concept of ownership, government's proper role of guaranteeing and protecting private property rights will only be secured when the liberals recognize the right of individual ownership.

In contrast to the liberals in Congress, the conservatives often make such statements as "if you don't have anything to hide, why should you be afraid of the government's knowing?" Thus, we find incompatibility between the conservatives' respect for economic freedom and limited government, and their disregard of personal privacy--one of the very foundations of the free society they often claim to support.

I maintain that freedom and privacy are inseparable elements in the philosophy of individual rights--the one held by this country's forefathers. Without privacy, there can be no assurance of freedom. Without the freedom to own property, and to further acquire it without using force or fraud, appeals for privacy are futile.

If the issue is as important as this, why does it seem that lawmakers and constituents are so uninterested in reversing the deadly trend toward ending financial privacy? In relatively calm conditions such as we are experiencing today, few believe they are really threatened by the state's intervention. The state's knowledge of every aspect of personal finances, some think, is inconsequential.

But, what about in emergency conditions? What happens if we find ourselves in a severe inflationary depression and all the world's monetary systems are in crises? What will the state do with the massive amounts of data collected on our finances then? Historically, when a state operates under emergency conditions, it is willing to "pull out all the stops" in order to insure its total victory. Centralization takes its toll and individuals then become aware of the profound importance of privacy. Their ability to protect and defend themselves and their property might depend on it. This is when citizens will regret their failure to fight back while they still had the opportunity.

Currently, though, people are predominately apathetic. When new legislation diminishing financial privacy is introduced, it is usually shoved through Congress, sometimes with only five minutes of debate on both sides. Furthermore, the short debate rarely centers on the issue of privacy and ownership. The dangerous parts of the legislation are usually stuck in obscure parts of the bill, and then safely wrapped in nebulous, bureaucratic language. Few take the time to examine the long-term impact of the legislation or care about the bill's effects on privacy.

This report tells a chilling tale. It's a tale which will shock those who have been, up to now, unaware of the incredible growth of "Big Brother" government. It skillfully cuts through the bureaucratic fog to perceptively analyze the grim status of financial privacy in America. One of the most surprising aspects of _The Closing Door_ is documentation of the incredible war the Reagan administration has waged on privacy. This is the administration which promised to "get the government off our back."

We cannot expect to regain our financial privacy until those representing us in Washington believe the issue is important to their constituents back home. At meetings in my home district, I can't remember a time when I was asked about my position on the government's knowledge of personal finances. Just think what would happen if a Congressman came home to meet with citizens in his district and found himself bombarded with questions on subjects such as off-shore banking, the Comprehensive Crime Control Act of 1984, or the power of the IRS. In such meetings, if ten people were there to ask questions like this, they would seem like an army to their local Congressman. He would then return to Washington and begin bringing the issue up to the forefront. I hope people will not wait for a national crisis to begin asking questions.

On a more fundamental level, financial privacy will not be restored until our society resolves the issue of rights and ownership. As long as the state continues to assert its ownership over all property and life, it will continue to trample on individual rights. Government needs a major overhaul, and people need to begin thinking about the role they want government to play in their lives. If people decide they value their privacy and freedom, then they must work for lasting long-term reforms.

The prospects for a reform of this magnitude are slim. In the meantime, begin protecting yourself and your family--now. The price of liberty, as in our Founding Fathers' time, is eternal vigilance against tyrannical government.

Dr. Ron Paul
Former Member of Congress

Chapter 1

The Dilemma: Constitutional Freedoms Under Attack

The citizen and legal resident of the United States today face a moral and philosophical dilemma unparalleled in the history of the Republic. The greatness of the nation has been essentially a product of the principles of liberty, as expounded by the founding fathers in the Constitution with its Bill of Rights. No student of government today can say that we are a free nation. The best we can say is that we are, in many areas, among the most free.

For the past 15 years basic freedoms have been under attack as never before. And the courts have, on the balance, supported this attack, holding that the destruction of the rights of the individual are subordinate to public need. The purpose of this report is to examine and reassess what we are permitting government to do to us under various guises and excuses.

First of all, we have to recognize that we have conditioned ourselves to focus our ire on the wrong people. We complain about the Gestapo-like tactics of the IRS, Department of Justice, Customs, Treasury, etc. Complaints that are, indeed, valid, as shall be seen later. However, remember that the awesome powers given to these agencies were not self-generated. While each creates its own administrative rules of enforcement, the powers to act are granted by Congress directly, as in the case of the infamous Bank Secrecy Act of 1970, or indirectly through permanent emergency powers delegated to the executive branch.

No matter what the source of the powers and authority, attacking basic individual liberties, the courts in recent years have, in the bulk of the cases, turned their backs on constitutional guarantees and held for the government and its agencies.

So, one is faced with the moral and philosophical dilemma cited at the beginning of this chapter. The entire principle of the Revolutionary War against England, and the Constitution that grew out of it, was that the rights of the individual supercede the power of government and that the function of the courts in our tri-partite system is to protect the individual's constitutional rights--not only from his fellow citizens but from government itself.

The problem is this: the average citizen who understands what is taking place in the dismantling of the Bill of Rights, on one hand, wants to be a loyal, law-abiding, patriot. On the other hand, can this person morally obey laws that undermine the very principles he or she was taught made this nation different and better than virtually all others in the world?

What is important to recognize is that this is not a conservative stance, a liberal stance or a libertarian stance. It criss-crosses all philosophical boundaries. For the conservative who sees the Constitution as a matter of strict construction, and who relies on the Founding Fathers' intent as the guiding philosophy for the nation, the emasculation of basic constitutional rights has to be a frightening and confusing element.

For the liberal who sees government as the benevolent protector and provider of welfare for all of its citizens, his philosophy is built around even further extensions of the principles of life, liberty and the pursuit of happiness as laid out in the Bill of Rights and expanded amendments. Thus, to the liberal, like the conservative, the tearing down of these guarantees by Congress, with the approval of the courts, has to be a matter of great concern.

There is also a little libertarian philosophy within virtually everyone, though one may not define oneself politically as Libertarian. Libertarian is derived from the word liberty and is a philosophy that emphasizes the individual's rights to do as he or she pleases, so long as force or fraud are not used. Because of this, one has to look at the emergence of monolithic government, creating laws that further repress the individual, as the hammer driving the final nails into the coffin of individual liberty.

Daily, one reads about various special interest groups trying to get government to do something or to stop something that someone else wants government to do. In dealing with this basic problem of individual constitutional rights, however, one comes up against the largest and most powerful of all special interest groups--the government itself.

The resolution of the question of whether this is still a government "of the people, by the people, and for the people" is one that should be of equal concern to conservatives, liberals and libertarians alike. Of the basic rights under attack and being systematically quashed in the United States, the most virulent and successful attacks have come upon the constitutional rights of privacy. It is clear that the Founding Fathers in their wildest imagination, could not have dreamed of the potentials of computers and electronic surveillance. So there was almost no case law and limited definition of privacy for most of the first 190 years of the existence of the Republic.

So, with little to work with historically, the courts have not been bothered with precedents in cases involving personal and financial privacy issues. Rather, they have struck out on their own and created a new body of law, basically holding that there are no constitutional guarantees in these areas.

In order to rectify this situation, the support of conservatives, liberals and libertarians alike will be necessary to create a clear-cut, definitive new constitutional amendment covering the scope of personal and financial privacy rights. As recently as July 1, 1985, the Supreme Court held that an unmarried couple living together in an apartment had a "constitutional right of privacy." Yet that same Court has held that one has no constitutional right of privacy relative to one's bank accounts, one's personal records, one's telephone, or even one's person at customs. Since one doesn't have this right to privacy, other Fourth and Fifth Amendment protections are also invalidated.

There is no question that unless something is done soon, the closing door on personal and financial privacy will be shut. And that is what this book is all about.

Chapter 2

The Bank Secrecy Act of 1970

From the lead paragraph of the June 1985 FORECASTS AND STRATEGIES NEWSLETTER, one gets a graphic picture: "The Reagan administration is pursuing a devastating, alarming assault on your personal and financial freedom. The threat has never been greater under any previous administration, Democrat or Republican. The new attack is evident everywhere: attorney's offices are being raided without warning, customs agents are searching passengers and issuing warnings about carrying cash when leaving the country, mail from abroad is being opened, bank tellers are being told to report 'suspicious transactions' to the Treasury Department."

This statement gives only a glimmer of the tip of the iceberg: The United States is accelerating into an Orwellian police state, making a mockery out of the constitutional guarantees of privacy, illegal search and seizure, and the protections from self-incrimination by removing that right from documents or information held by third parties.

The writers of the Constitution did not contemplate the effects of the electronic age, neither its capacity for surveillance nor its ability to record vast amounts of data on computers. Thus, the isolated early cases involving privacy were built around invasion of the privacy of a man's castle, his home, or his physical person. So there was little, if anything, in the cornerstone of privacy law that could by attributed back to Justice Oliver Wendell Holmes, to John Marshall, or even to the great appellate judge, Learned Hand, concerning modern, electronic surveillance capabilities.

Thus, when the Treasury Department in 1970 asked Congress for, and got, the Bank Secrecy Act of 1970, the first major step was taken toward electronic surveillance of U.S. citizens on a large scale. The courts, in handling the cases that arose from the Act, in essence operated on a premise that since no precedents existed, they could rewrite the Constitution. It was a whole new ball game. In most of the early Supreme Court cases, Justice William O. Douglas dissented vigorously, but the disposition of the Court in every decision supported the government's "right" to know everything about the individual as covered by the Act.

It is important to know and understand the Bank Secrecy Act. All of the more onerous legislative powers granted to federal agencies in this area have grown out of this act. The Supreme Court's decision that third party reporting requirements do not violate one's personal constitutional right of privacy, or the Fourth and Fifth Amendments, has been based on it.

In the first place, the very name is misleading. It is the kind of political brainwashing that is used to make the public feel that something that is bad is good, or to engender a lack of interest until it is too late. The fact is the Bank Secrecy Act is exactly the opposite of what the name implies. It is the legislative end to bank secrecy. According to the authoritative LAW OF FINANCIAL PRIVACY, by L. Richard Fischer, published in 1983, "On the contrary, its main purpose is to avoid secrecy by requiring financial institutions to maintain records and submit reports that federal agencies may use . . ."

What were the conditions prior to the Bank Secrecy Act? For all practical purposes, since banks did not have to maintain records beyond their own specific operational needs, in the interest of profitability there was a concerted effort on the part of the banking industry to reduce administrative paperwork by keeping record maintenance to a minimum. In addition, it took substantive search warrants to even get at what was there. The person with international interests could conduct overseas business without anyone knowing it. In the framework of reality, there was a high level of banking secrecy operative in the U.S. without the need for a banking secrecy-type law.

At the behest of the Treasury Department, and backed by other agencies, the Bank Secrecy Act was made into law. The bank un-secrecy act was what it become. What did this Act put into the law that began the legislative dismantling of personal financial privacy? It established the following powers:

1. The requirement that any citizen, resident or business in the U.S. report or record transactions with foreign financial agencies.

2. The requirement that any person who transports, or causes to be transported, in excess of $5,000 in U.S. currency or monetary instruments be reported.

3. The Secretary of the Treasury was given broad powers to specify the circumstances under which a myriad of institutions must report domestic and foreign transactions in currency or monetary instruments.

4. The Secretary is empowered to require financial and other institutions to keep microfilm or other records of each check draft, or similar instrument that is drawn on or received by them, to maintain records of the identities of account holders, and the identities of persons engaging in reportable transactions pursuant to the Currency and Foreign Transactions Reporting Act of 1953.

5. The Secretary also may make record-keeping rules for issuers of travelers checks and credit cards, international transfer agents, currency exchanges and other similar businesses. (This really is part of 4, but important enough to separate out.)

At this stage, the power of the government to compel involuntary record-keeping by virtually every type of institution that deals in monetary instruments, and the power to compel automatic reporting of that information in certain instances and involuntary reporting, on demand, in all others was in place.

What makes it worse is that Congress did not attempt to deal with potential abuses by creating restraints or guidelines on the authority of the Secretary of the Treasury to enforce the Act. With minor exceptions, the Secretary has almost unlimited powers to promulgate regulations involving both civil and criminal penalties against institutions that fail to cooperate. On criminal penalties, only the word "willful" is used as a limitation. And as shall be seen later on, the courts in these matters have virtually defined willful as merely doing it.

If one wanted to sympathize with the purported excuse for the creation of this incredible invasion of privacy law, it would be hard to do so in the light of due process of law. Philosophically one can sympathize with a premise that law and order is more difficult to maintain in a free society than in a police state dictatorship. But, one cannot sympathize with the police state premise that suppresses crime by suppressing everybody.

The ostensible purpose of the Bank Secrecy Act is to create access to records that will help the government convict individuals of crimes under investigation; records or information of a financial nature that will prove the payment for, or intent to defraud, factors in the case. Nowhere in this Act is there a limitation on the information that can be demanded of an institution if some criminal action against an individual has been instituted, or if probable cause for action exists. It is a carte blanche fishing-trip mandate, aimed at every citizen in the country, regardless of the government's claim of using it only as a tool against crime.

In addition to his authority over domestic financial institutions, the Secretary of the Treasury also has the authority to force individuals to report relationships with, as well as maintain records of, any transactions with foreign financial institutions. The individual must do this by both filling out Form 90-22-1 and reporting any foreign bank accounts on Form 1040.

The regulations as produced by the Treasury Department also place the onus on individuals to report the transport of $5,000 or more in currency or other monetary instruments. This includes the mailing of such funds or instruments. Incidentally, in the Crime Control Act of 1984, the amount was raised to $10,000, but even more vicious enforcement regulations have gone along with this increase. Understand this: The individual to whom the money or instrument belongs is not the only one who is liable. Quoting from the Act itself: "For this purpose, a person is deemed to have caused the transportation, mailing or shipping if he aids, abets, counsels, commands, procures or requests it to be done by a financial institution or any other person."

Whatever exceptions to the above exist in the present regulations, these are not permanent limitations. The Secretary's authority, as just quoted, is without limitation on his power to issue enforcement regulations.

The following outline shows the extent to which the Bank Secrecy Act with amendments has been promulgated into regulation. It is important to remember that the power to regulate is practically limitless.

1. Mandatory reporting requirement.

   (a) Any currency transaction in an amount greater than $10,000

      (1) Certain types of retail business and withdrawals of regular payrolls, etc., are exempted, but records must be maintained by the bank.

2. Mandatory record-keeping to be reported.

   (a) Name, address, purpose and other information on credit extensions in excess of $5,000.

   (b) Any domestic transfer or credit in excess of $10,000.

   (c) Transfers or credits to a person, account or place outside of the United States in excess of $10,000. And receipts therefrom.

      (1) Transfer to an account in the U.S. where the bank knows the account's address is outside the U.S. is considered a foreign transfer.

(2) Wire transfers not included in present law.

3. Mandatory record-keeping to be retained.

(a) Customer information on all bank account including tax I.D. number is required. Some minor levels of confidentiality have been placed on this information by Congress.

(b) A copy of each transaction in excess of $100 must be retained by the bank from whom it has been drawn.

(1) Records necessary to reconstruct a demand deposit account must be held for two years and all other records for five years.

The Bank Secrecy Act was amended in 1981 (31 CFR #103.35 and forward) to extend the same rules of record-keeping to brokers and dealers in securities. Since then, additional amendments bringing coin and bullion dealers under the Act have also been passed and effected.

Federal bank regulators, the Securities and Exchange Commission, and Customs specifically regulate their areas of the Act, and the Internal Revenue Service administers any portion that the others do not. The penalties that the enforcers have to work with are so powerful that it is not difficult to get compliance from most financial institutions and their employees. Civil penalties for both institutions and employees start at $1,000. Reporting violations that also involve the commission or facilitation of another crime can lead to statutory fines as high as

$500,000, imprisonment up to five years, or both. A false report is punishable by up to $10,000 and/or five years in prison. This is pretty strong medicine for the poor bank employee to stand up against.

How do the courts view the Bank Secrecy Act? There are three landmark cases: California Banks Association vs. Shultz, 416 US 21 (1974); U.S. vs. Miller, 425 US 435 (1976); and Fisher vs. U.S., 425 US 391 (1976). Without going into lengthy discourse, these cases set precedents that, without substantial changes in the law itself or constitutional redefinition of privacy, make further challenge improbable.

The decision in the Bankers case virtually wiped out any possible Fifth Amendment protection against self-incrimination in the use of bank records. In essence, the case held that the records were, in fact, the records of the bank used in the course of its business, and therefore the bank could not invoke the rights of the customer as a reason to refuse to disclose the records. Because the banks were themselves involved in the transactions, their records were subject to demands made by the regulatory agencies.

In essence, the decision created an enormous precedent. The bank's records of an individual's transactions do not belong to the individual but, rather, are the property of the bank. Thus, in the Miller case, when a depositor came to court to object to the subpoena of his records from his bank, using the Bankers Association case as a precedent, it was all over before it began. The Miller court said that the depositor could assert neither possession nor ownership of the documents in question, thereby precluding any right to privacy based on property interests.

Secondly, a depositor's expectations of privacy were negated by the fact that the checks were, in essence, published when placed in the banking cycle. Any information contained in the checks was voluntarily conveyed to the banks and exposed to their employees in the ordinary course of business. As a result, the depositor, in revealing his affairs to another, took the "risk" that the information would be conveyed by that person to the government. Therefore, what a person knowingly exposes to the public is not subject to Fourth Amendment protection, and such information can be obtained by the government without infringing upon any privacy right.

The subpoena issue of the Fisher case was widely quoted in the Miller decision, the essence found in 425 US 444 said, "A subpoena to a third party to obtain the records of the party does not violate the rights of a defendant, even in the midst of a criminal prosecution."

In essense, then, there are no constitutional guarantees protected in the Bank Secrecy Act. If the records don't belong to the individual, one has no rights relevant to them. Even worse, in practice, these records are available to any other agency or department of the federal government upon request to the Secretary. The request merely need state the information desired, the criminal, tax or regulatory proceeding for which the information is sought, and the official need for such information. The requesting agency is supposed to keep the information confidential except for "official purposes." Who can define that?

For records maintained but not reportable to the Secretary, legal process is required. What this means is that other agencies that have congressionally-imposed limitations on their investigative powers now have access to information to which they were formerly restricted by Fourth and Fifth Amendment considerations.

This problem did concern Congress, and while what it did was shot full of loopholes, the result was the Right to Privacy Act of 1978--to be examined next. Be aware however, the elements of the Crime Control Act of 1984, and certain legislation currently pending in Congress, threaten to undermine the few protections that do exist in the Right to Privacy Act.

Chapter 3

The Financial Privacy Act of 1978

In the period following the California Bankers Association, Miller and Fisher cases, Congress had a moment of soul-searching. Some members of Congress were appalled by the Court's rulings as to the inapplicability of Fourth and Fifth Amendment protections. These legislators feared government misuse of individuals' personal financial records held by financial institutions. As a result, in 1978, the last-ditch fight to restore some vestiges of personal financial privacy was fought and lost.

In essence, the 1974 and 1978 acts did not in any way restore the privacy of the records held by institutions from the eyes of government. In fact, these acts legitimized the interest of the Bank Secrecy Act by accepting its requirements as valid and constitutional. All that these acts accomplished was to attempt to establish some procedures relative to interagency exchanges of information, the right to see and challenge the content of such information, and the procedures to be followed by the government in obtaining such information.

As shall be seen, the acts are so full of exceptions that, for all practical purposes, whatever minor protection they grant, these are easily outweighed by those exceptions. Even worse, the notice provisions, as they exist, are currently under attack in Congress as being an impediment to effective law enforcement.

This examination will begin with a look at the Privacy Act of 1974. First, the right of one agency to get information on an individual from another agency will be dealt with:

> "Sec. #200,255 - Conditions of Disclosure. No agency shall disclose any record which is contained in a system of records to any person or to another agency, except pursuant to a written request by, or with the prior written consent of, the individual to whom the record pertains, unless disclosure of the record would be . . ."

It starts out sounding wonderful. Then comes the list of exceptions, covering every probable reason why a government agency would desire financial records and information, except perhaps for a loan or grant which the person himself is seeking from the government.

The big catchall, which doesn't even require a court order, makes any kind of fishing trip based on supposition possible. That is embodied in number (7) of the exceptions.

> "(7) To another agency or to an instrumentality of any governmental jurisdiction within or under the control of the United States for a civil or criminal law enforcement activity if the activity is authorized by law, and if the head of the agency or instrumentality has made a written request to the agency which maintains the record specifying the particular portion desired and the

law enforcement activity for which the record is sought."

So much for the need for the individual's written consent to the transfer of the records between agencies.

Other areas covered by the 1974 Act are as follows:

1. Agencies must maintain accounting records of who, what, why and when records were turned over by them to someone else. (200,261)

2. Agencies must comply with requests of individuals to know if records about them are held by an agency; to permit him to see those records, and to request amendment of the records if he disagrees with them. However, this right is abrogated if the information was compiled in reasonable anticipation of a civil action or proceeding. (200,265)

3. Rules of conduct for the agency that is holding records. (200,271)

4. Procedures for handling inquiries. (200,275)

5. Civil remedies available to individuals for failure of an agency to comply with the rules. Unlike most tax cases, attorney fees are recoverable. (200,281)

6. Exceptions. (200,295) (200,301)

   a. CIA
   b. Any criminal law enforcement agency
   c. Statistical services
   d. Federal employment applications

7. Records, when purpose is completed, to be stored in national archives.

Thus, in the 1974 Act one sees that indiscriminate exchanges of information between government agencies is curtailed to some extent. The following basic precepts are created. An individual is supposed to be notified if his records are requested from one agency by another, and further has the right of inquiry as to what records agencies hold. However, there are so many exceptions as to when notification can be withheld, or information withheld when requested of an agency, that few people can get to the information the government has.

Now let us look at the Right to Financial Privacy Act of 1978. The intent of Congress in proposing the legislation was excellent. The three basic purposes expressed were:

1. To require that customers be notified before disclosure of their records to the government.
2. To give customers the right to challenge the release of their records to the government.
3. To require government to document disclosure of information in customer records to itself as well as interagency transfers of that information to give the customer a paper trail to follow.

What came out of the hopper after lobbying by the Department of Justice and the banking industry, which did not desire any responsibility to the customer, was a bill that gave a surface appearance of addressing those principles. In reality it protects nobody from the government's ability to get any records it wants, and in most cases, without notification really being needed.

One needs to deal with a few definitions of who is involved in these protections, such as they are. First, a "customer" can only be an individual or a partnership of not more than five partners. This means no protective procedures at all exist for corporations, estates, many forms of trusts or trustees, and the account must be maintained in the customer's name. Section 12 USC 3401(1) defines what kind of institutions are subject to compliance with the 1978 Act. It also reconfirms the government's authority to elicit information from those institutions, albeit with some procedural limitations created by the Act. Those defined are:

1. Banks
2. Savings Banks
3. Card Issuers (credit card companies including store or gasoline cards)
4. Industrial Loan Companies
5. Trust Companies
6. Savings & Loan, Building & Loan, etc.
7. Credit Unions
8. Consumer Finance Institutions

Though securities and commodities brokers and bullion dealers have been placed under extensions of the Bank Secrecy Act's reporting and record-keeping regulations, they are not as yet covered by the Right to Financial Privacy Act.

The methods, which are available to government agencies to obtain the desired information about the customer from these financial institutions, fall into two categories. The first of these is the search warrant, which requires no notice to the customer. The second is a group of methods consisting of customer authorization, administrative subpoenas or summonses, judicial subpoenas or formal written requests which require advance notice to the customer and the opportunity to challenge the request for information.

Probably the single greatest real benefit to the public in the 1978 Act is that part requiring written customer authorization to the institution to turn over his records to the government. Many institutions before the Act were trying to force customers to sign open-end blanket authorizations allowing the bank to reveal their records, at the request of the government, as a condition of doing business. Many stuck it in the fine print of a loan agreement, etc. This sort of coercion and trickery were rendered illegal. The customer now can only give a written authorization for specific information and for not more than three months. In addition, this authorization can be revoked prior to the records being turned over.

Originally, the Act was written to force the government to go to court to prove it needed the records, if the customer filed a written objection with the financial institution. This was changed to put the whole burden on the customer. The customer now has ten days after receipt of service, or fourteen days from date of mailing of the notice by the government, to respond in Federal Court or else the financial institution must turn over the records. What makes this procedure devastating, even if it is followed in every instance, is the "Formal

Written Request" in Section 1108 of the Act. Even if the agency cannot prove sufficient probable cause to get a judicial or administrative subpoena or summons, it can still go after the records with a mere written request to the bank. The customer has the burden of going to a Federal Court within ten days to try to prevent the records from being turned over.

Even if the government had to religiously follow these procedures in all cases, which it doesn't, as shall be seen in a moment, the individual still has very little chance of success in court. Again, going back to the Miller and Fisher decisions, once a person goes to court, he becomes subject to the ruling that he has no Fourth or Fifth Amendment rights relative to the records which financial institutions hold and maintain under the Bank Secrecy Act.

However, it gets worse. Under section 1109 of the Act, the government can apply to an appropriate court for a delay of ninety days in the notification of the customer if the presiding judge or magistrate finds that:

1. The investigation being conducted is within the lawful jurisdiction of the government authority seeking the financial records.

2. There is reason to believe that the records being sought are relevant to a legitimate law enforcement inquiry; and

3. There is reason to believe that such notice will result in

   a. Endangering life or physical safety of any person

b. Flight from prosecution
c. Destruction of or tampering with evidence
d. Intimidation of potential witnesses
e. Otherwise seriously jeopardizing an investigation or official proceeding or unduly delaying a trial or ongoing official proceeding to the same extent as the circumstances in the preceding subparagraphs.

Thus, the mechanism exists for the entire system of notice, which is the heart of the Act, to be abrogated--and easily so. Pursuant to Section 1110 of the Act, the challenge procedures described earlier represent the "sole judicial remedy available to a customer to oppose disclosure of financial records pursuant to this title."

This is of little help when the records have been obtained by search warrant carrying an automatic delay of ninety days before notification or by ninety-day judicial delay under Section 1109. The fact is the government can have one's records for 90 days before a person even knows about it.

If one is wondering at this point just how much privacy there is in the Right to Financial Privacy Act of 1978, Section 1113 of the Act, titled "Exceptions", will list but a few of the more pertinent exceptions:

(b) Nothing in this title prohibits examination by or disclosure to any supervisory agency of financial records or information in the exercise of its supervisory, regulatory or monetary functions with a financial institution.

(c) Nothing in this title prohibits the disclosure of financial records in accordance with procedures authorized by the Internal Revenue Code.

(d) Nothing in this title shall authorize the withholding of financial records or information required to be reported in accordance with any Federal statute or rules promulgated thereunder.

(e) Nothing in this title shall apply when financial records are sought by a Government authority under the Federal Rules of Civil or Criminal Procedure or comparable rules of other courts in connection with litigation to which the Government authority and the customer are parties.

There are more exceptions under Section 1113, but the examples given are enough to give anyone the impression that the Act is full of holes. No one can seriously consider it a financial privacy law.

Another aspect of the Act, which is absolutely mind-boggling, is the lack of value that Congress places upon an invasion of a person's privacy by the government in illegally or improperly obtaining or disclosing information. Section 1117 of the Act imposes a $100 fine on the agency or institution found guilty or wrongdoing "without regard to the volume of records involved." Compare this to penalties up to $500,000 that can be imposed on a citizen for the mere failure to submit a form or to answer a question that the government may require. That in itself is a good measure of how little regard government has for the privacy rights of individuals.

The original intent of Congress in creating a financial privacy act in 1978 was to engender a greater level of concern for the individual's rights within the court system, when the government was seeking the financial records of a particular bank's or similar institution's customers. Thus, the idea was to insert some privacy rights for the citizen into the process. The weakness of this legislation has already been discussed. Next, it is important to look at what the courts have ruled when the government's acts in requesting or obtaining records have been challenged through the judicial system.

In Clayton Brokerage Co. vs. Clement, 87 FRD 569 (D.Md. 1980), the court held that the Financial Privacy Act did not preclude discovery of a customer's bank transactions in a civil suit, and that a subpoena to obtain the records did not violate "any cognizable privacy right of the defendant." The court also stated that the defendant lacked standing to assert issues of lack of relevance and estoppel because the records belonged to the bank.

In the U.S. vs. MacKay, 608F, 2nd 830 (1979), the customer asserted that the IRS failed to comply with the Right to Financial Privacy Act in seeking the customer's records. The court held that both the legislative history and the expressed terms of the Financial Privacy Act make it clear that the Act does not override the power to summons contained in the Internal Revenue Code.

And again in U.S. vs. Wills, 475 F. Supp. 492 (M.D. Fla. 1979), the court held that neither the Financial Privacy Act nor the Freedom of Information Act had any application to the enforcement of IRS summonses or to the restriction of enforcement.

One of the alleged main protections of the Act is to prevent a bank from releasing records without the government presenting (to the bank) a certificate of compliance with the Act. Despite this, in U.S. vs. Wills, the court held that the Financial Privacy Act does not prohibit disclosure under the Internal Revenue Code, and thus that the provisions of 12 USC 3403b (certificate of compliance requirement) have no application to the enforcement of IRS summonses.

As one can see here, the Right to Financial Privacy Act of 1978 may have been a result of good intentions by Congress designed to address some of the patent abuses of the Bank Secrecy Act of 1970. But, the reality is that the courts have been heavily slanted in interpretation towards the rights of the government over the rights of the citizen. In addition, the Act has so many exceptions that it does little to protect personal financial privacy. In fact, as was said at the beginning of the chapter, if anything, it legitimizes the search and seizure by government of personal financial records.

The 1978 Act, thus, represents Congress' last feeble effort towards some vestige of protecting financial privacy.

Chapter 4

TEFRA 1982

The Tax Equity and Fiscal Responsibility Act of 1982, plus 1983 amendments, known as TEFRA, drastically expanded the areas of records accessible to government, particularly the Internal Revenue Service. The three major thrusts of the Act were as follows:

1. To increase access to third party records through administrative summons by including the following as accessible record-keepers; banks, trust companies, credit unions, mutual savings banks, cooperative banks, other savings institutions chartered under Federal or State laws, consumer reporting agencies (such as credit bureaus), credit card issuers including merchants, brokers, attorneys, accountants, and barter exchanges.

2. To extend the use of the administrative summons to criminal investigation and not just administrative procedure or tax deficiency information.

3. Attacks offshore investors by increasing fines for failure to file information returns on foreign corporations; expands the number of people required to file returns on foreign personal holding companies, extends court summons to people living abroad; empowers courts to prohibit admission of evidence submitted by persons who fail to comply with documents requests.

The administrative summons, probably the most awesome power ever granted to any government agency in modern times, was essentially a tool of the Tax Reform Act of

1976. The 1976 Act was passed because of the Miller and Fisher cases. These cases left the citizen with no Fourth Amendment rights to challenge seizure under the Bank Secrecy Act. Under the 1976 Act, notification had to be given to the customer of the intent to request his records. The customer could file an objection with the financial institution, and the burden of instituting litigation fell upon the IRS.

In discussing the Right to Financial Privacy Act (1978) in the last chapter, this was not the case in the instances of court-issued subpoenas or summonses. There, the burden of instituting litigation fell upon the citizen. But the Right to Financial Privacy Act did not shift the burden in the case of the administrative summons. Now, in all cases of IRS requests for third-party information, the entire burden of instituting court action to prevent the records from being turned over, falls upon the citizen.

The IRS administrative summons will be analyzed in greater depth in Chapter 6. However, it will be referenced in this chapter, as most of the cases in which TEFRA was challenged occurred as a result of the summons. The areas that were clearly defined as being legitimate targets for third-party record requests, extending previous definitions, were consumer reporting agencies, brokers, attorneys, accountants, and barter exchanges.

1. CONSUMER REPORTING AGENCIES. Prior to the 1976 act in U.S. vs. Puntorieri, 379 F. Supp. 332,734 (1974), the court ruled that the IRS had to obtain a court order or the consumer's consent to obtain consumer reports in the hands of a consumer reporting agency. After the 1976 act in U.S. vs. Citibank, m-18-304 (SDNY 1980), the court held that the IRS should be able to obtain records from consumer reporting agencies through use of a valid summons without a court order or the customer's written instruction. Before TEFRA this could only be used for tax information or liability. After TEFRA it was available for criminal inquiry (TEFRA * 353(a)IRC * 7602(b)).

2. BROKERS. The tax bill of 1982 (TEFRA) contained instructions to the Secretary of the Treasury to write regulations requiring brokers to report all trades, thereby enabling the IRS to monitor capital gains on those trades. In March 1983, IRC Sec. 6045 was announced:

> "(a) General Rule: Every person doing business as a broker shall, when required by the Secretary, make a return, in accordance with such regulations as the Secretary may prescribe, showing the name and address of each customer, with such details regarding gross proceeds and such other information as the Secretary may by forms or regulations require with respect to such business."

The format is a form 1099 which requires reporting on a transactional basis, rather than year-end, which is the format for reporting interest, dividends, etc. All trades on securities, bond, and commodities markets were clearly covered by this act. But the Treasury has seen fit to extend the IRS authority to bullion dealers, despite the fact that they buy and resell for their own accounts and are not technically brokers. Leveraged contracts on silver and gold are clearly covered. While numismatic coins are apparently not specifically covered by current regulations, in this regard, there is no room for complacency among coin or other collectables dealers for the future.

3. ATTORNEYS AND ACCOUNTANTS. In many respects this is the area that has been most hard hit by the unconstrained extension of the government's right to invade the individual's personal financial privacy. For generations, the Common Law concept of privilege of information has been the cornerstone of the confidential relationship between attorney and client. In more recent years this same privilege has been upheld relative to an accountant-client relationship. How can a client possibly work with an accountant unless the accountant has access to the client's most confidential financial records? In Matter vs. Newton, 718 F. 2nd 1015 (1983), the court held that absent an explicit congressional grant of privilege (for accountants) the court cannot impose additional restrictions on the grant of summons power to the IRS in 26 USC 7602.

4. BARTER EXCHANGES. The barter exchange is an enigma for government record-keepers. Since these types of

exchanges deal "in kind" rather than through paper transactions, generally no bank, credit card or personal records exist. Only the barter exchange keeps records of the transactions and of its members. There are two important cases where the IRS has used the John Doe format of summons to get the third party information from barter exchanges.

In re: Tax Liabilities of John Does, Members of the Columbus Trade Exchange 671 7.2nd 799 (1982). In this instance, the IRS gave as the basis of its summons the audited tax returns of members of similar barter exchanges in which the IRS had found evidence of improper reporting practices. On this basis it sought to audit members of the Columbus Trade Exchange. The district court held that it was merely a fishing expedition and the IRS had not complied with the "Reasonable basis for belief" requirement. This ruling was overturned by the Sixth Circuit Appeals Court, which held that the "reasonable basis for belief" requirement was satisfied by demonstrating the high incidence of tax violations in a similar barter organization.

In Kroll vs. United States, 573 F. Supp. 982 (1983), the court put the burden on the taxpayer to prove undisputed facts involving the IRS's intent to identify customers of the National Commodity and Barter Exchange for purposes of establishing tax liability. Obviously this rationale is faulty as there is no way for the taxpayer to prove intent until after the fact of an audit.

One of the most questionable areas in the development of the entire line of legislative and court decisions attacking personal financial privacy is that which makes non-payment or non-reporting of taxes a major criminal matter. In most of the world, such a crime involves only civil liability. In the United States, penalties for non-reporting, onus reporting etc., are, for the most part, more severe than those for burglary, manslaughter, rape, drugs, or major white collar crime. This subject will be covered in greater depth in Chapter 6.

However, under TEFRA, Revised Sec. 7602(b), the extension of the use of the IRS administrative summons for criminal investigation violates one of our basic precepts of criminal law. Search and seizure statutes have always required the police or investigative agency to show due cause to a court in order to procure a subpoena, a warrant or a summons. The protection of this separation of Executive and Judicial branches has always been the cornerstone of this country's legal process, a means of protecting ordinary citizens from over zealous police actions.

Under TEFRA, the IRS, without any authority other than itself to rule on the validity of its summons, can now use this weapon to inquire into criminal conduct, even if the criminal conduct is the sole object of the investigation. What a horrible potential tool for harassment against any who disagree with the administration in power.

The explanation for the change is cited in 97th Congress 2nd Session 236. There, the Joint Committee on Taxation stated, "Under prior law, the use of the administrative summons is limited to determination and collection of taxes. The act expands this authority to include the right to issue a summons for the purpose of inquiring into any offense connected with the administration or enforcement of the Internal Revenue laws, even when the criminal investigation is the sole investigation."

Since the administrative summons can be served on third party record-keepers (banks, attorneys, accountants, etc.), privacy can now be invaded in a criminal investigation, without either court approval or any tax liability having been established. One can hardly doubt that this represents the most awesome police investigative power ever granted.

The principles of using the administrative summons in criminal investigations versus various objections have been continually upheld by the courts. Without citing the details of the decisions, one's attention is called to <u>Garpeg, Ltd. vs. United States</u>, (8401 USTC 9439 SD NY 1984); <u>Goodwin vs. United States</u> (564 F. Supp. 1209 D Del.

1983), Kroll vs. United States, (573 F. Supp. 982 ND Ind. 1983) and Gluck vs. United States, (83-1523 D NJ 1983).

The third general area of TEFRA deals with overseas investment by U.S. citizens, corporations, or residents. Since the U.S. is one of only two countries in the world that claims a tax right on the income of its citizens, earned or unearned, created beyond the borders of the country, there has been a growing paranoia about the use of tax havens by Americans. This subject will be dealt with in depth in Chapter 8.

However, with fines up to $400,000 and jail penalties for failure to properly answer questions on the 90-22 form on foreign bank accounts, trusts, and corporations, the tactic of fear of punishment has been injected as a lever to force citizens to give up the privacy of foreign investment in secrecy havens.

While TEFRA expands the number of people who are required to report and the penalties for failure to do so, the two most important changes in the law were the following:

1. Previously, permanent residents of foreign jurisdictions could not be served for purposes of obtaining records and evidence as they had no domicile under the jurisdiction of a Federal Court. Now they can be served in the Federal District Court for the District of Columbia for purposes of establishing civil or criminal jurisdiction. This, in effect, destroys the ability of a citizen to have freedom of choice to live abroad, out of the jurisdiction of the U.S.

Government's power to prosecute in tax matters.

2. Refusal of an individual to comply with an order to produce personal overseas financial records precludes the use of those records in a future court hearing as a defense. What this means by analogy is that, while in a murder case new evidence can be submitted at any time, even on appeal as a basis for a new trial, in a tax matter mere failure to comply with an IRS demand for information renders that information useless as a defense later. In short, tax non-compliance is considered a more vicious crime than murder.

To summarize, what are the net effects of the Tax Equity and Fiscal Responsibility Act of 1982 (TEFRA)?

1. Virtually no person with whom a taxpayer's records are stored is immune to a summons to deliver those records to the IRS. Attorney-client and accountant-client privilege is effectively destroyed.

2. The IRS, with no court overview, can issue administrative summons to try to establish a criminal case without even establishing tax liability.

3. Fines and penalties for failure to provide information on offshore activities are jacked up, the District of Columbia is established as the jurisdiction for service on offshore residents, and fundamental rules of evidence in our jurisprudence system are overturned by making records refused to the IRS inadmissable in court at a future hearing.

THE CLOSING DOOR

Chapter 5

Comprehensive Crime Control Act of 1984

The legislation discussed in the previous four chapters dealt primarily with areas of invasions of personal financial privacy. These were characterized by court approved acts which, in essence, meant that, in whatever place records of financial transactions might be stored, those records were accessible to government agencies for criminal or civil prosecution against the individual.

The courts held that such records were exempt from the constitutional right of privacy, and that neither the holder of the records nor the individual to whom they relate have any Fourth or Fifth Amendment rights to protect them from the seizure or the use of those records by the government.

The Comprehensive Crime Control Act of 1984 has broadened the scope of areas in which personal privacy can be invaded by government. However, beyond this broadening of scope, the act again raises the serious question: is there any limit to the extent government can go to destroy, in its entirety, the principles of the Bill of Rights of the United States Constitution? The courts are seemingly holding that the end justifies the means, and that, where it is government versus the ordinary citizen, the Constitution is not applicable to the rights of the citizen.

The Act of 1984 created the following new problems involving the rights of privacy of the individual:

1. It gave the U.S. Customs Service the right to search without a warrant on mere suspicion.

2. It gave the U.S. Customs Service the right to open the mails without a warrant on mere suspicion.

3. It made overseas movements of money a crime in itself and authorized wire taps without a warrant on those suspected of planning to move money.

4. It raised the penalty for failure to report movements in excess of $10,000 from a $1,000 fine and/or one year in jail, to $250,000 in fines and/or five years in prison.

5. It made use of the greatest tool of the Gestapo: paid informers.

The ostensible purpose of these provisions is to combat the laundering of money by drug smugglers or other perpetrators involved in organized crime. Unfortunately, the provisions of the Act were not written in a way wholly consistent with this purpose. If these same provisions were written to carry with them proper verbiage such as "upon certification of the Attorney General that a bona fide suspicion or investigation of an individual for some aspect of organized crime, including drugs, was in process," it would then serve to define the purpose of the Act into the law.

In its present form, the Act makes the transportation of money the crime. This means every person who wants to make an offshore purchase or diversify his holdings offshore, must report any movement of funds in excess of $10,000 or be branded a criminal. Some of the sections of the Act that clearly impinge upon the constitutional rights of the individual are, as follows:

> "Section 589 - Arrest authority of Customs officers.
>
> (3) Make an arrest with a warrant . . . for a felony cognizable under the laws of the United States committed outside the officer's presence if the officer has reasonable grounds to believe that the person to be arrested has committed . . . a felony."

Again, one gets into the jury areas of the Fourth Amendment protections against illegal search and seizure. A great concern of both the Founding Fathers and the courts over the years has been abuse of police powers. Except where the police official is himself witness to, or in support of others who were witness to, a crime in which hot pursuit is required to apprehend a suspect, the warrant is the basic protection against arbitrary police power. To grant arrest authority on "reasonable belief" without a warrant makes an officer an umpire. It is the court that should have the role of umpire to determine reasonable belief. The officer's role is to execute the will of the court once the warrant is issued.

With modern technology, any such cases should be readily accessible in the computers at any Customs station. The suspect can always be detained long enough to make the check without violating his rights. Arrest without a warrant is an infringement on the constitutional rights of the individual.

"Subsection (a) of Section 5322 of Title 31 United States Code is amended by striking out $1,000 or imprisonment not more than one year, or both, and inserting in lieu thereof $250,000, or imprisonment not more than five years, or both."

Again, this might be in order if directly tied to an indictment and conviction for acts of organized crime including drug dealing. In short, a conviction for a major crime against other citizens, also involving unreported movements of currency or negotiable instruments, could properly carry substantial penalties.

Instead, the act, in itself, of transporting unreported sums in excess of $10,000 has become classified as a major penal offense. The imputation that any person who desires to remove personal funds from the jurisdiction of the United States for reasons of personal privacy is a criminal, strikes heavily at the Fifth Amendment rights against self-incrimination. Where there is no criminal intent, why should the ordinary citizen have his rights to personal privacy brought under attack with penalties so fearsome that he is forced to subject himself to unwelcome reporting requirements.

Hasn't fear been the explicit tool of dictatorships from the beginning of time? Where is the nation going when one is subjected to $400,000 fines for failure to answer a question on a form? Or $250,000 fines for failure to report monetary transactions involving overseas movements of money? And, again, these weapons of fear and terror are, in fact, aimed at every citizen, not just the criminal element in the nation's midst.

Subsection (b) of Section 5316 of Title 31 is added:

> "A Customs office may stop and search, without a search warrant, a vehicle, vessel, aircraft, or other conveyance, envelope or other container, or person entering or departing the United States with respect to which or whom the officer has reasonable cause to believe there is a monetary instrument being transported in violation of section 5316 of this Title."

If nothing heretofore has proved frightening, this certainly should cause concern. The only limitation on total search of every envelope, package, or piece of luggage entering or leaving the United States is the number of enforcement officers that are authorized to be hired by the Treasury Department. Orwell's "Big Brother" is becoming alarmingly real in this country. That Congress could grant such power to open and search the mails without a warrant, is a tremendous blow to the concepts of privacy from anyone's standpoint. And, no one must apologize or pay any penalty if a person's mail, luggage, or person is wrongfully searched. Where are the outer limits in the government's pursuit of the destruction of privacy? Is everyone to be made into a criminal for refusing to tell all?

What has always been the principal tool of the closed society? The answer is, turning neighbor against neighbor by offering rewards to informants. This is exactly what the Comprehensive Crime Control Act of 1984 does. A new section, 5323, is added to Title 19:

> "Section 5323 - Rewards for Informants.
>
> (a) The Secretary may pay a reward to an individual who provides information which leads to a recovery of criminal fine, civil penalty, or forfeiture which exceeds $50,000 for a violation of this chapter.
>
> (b) The Secretary shall determine the amount of a reward under this Section. The Secretary may not award more than 25 per centum of the net amount of the fine, penalty, or forfeiture collected or $150,000, whichever is less."

Isn't it amazing? There are titles in the Act dealing with drugs and drug dealers, but nowhere are there provisions for rewards for information leading to the apprehension of real criminals. Unfortunately, however, this is not true in the area of citizens' transporting funds overseas. In such cases, informants can reap hugh rewards for information that results in arrest and conviction.

It's this precedent that everyone should fear. Again, no penalty is provided against the malicious neighbor who might turn an individual over to the authorities purely for spite. If government can create a system of informants at this level, what comes next? Will one's neighbors be rewarded for turning a person in for every possible discrepancy involving personal financial matters? Remember again, neither drugs nor organized crime is a target here. The rewards are offered to help prevent the individual from moving private property to or from a chosen location, without reporting the act.

Finally, Section 2516 of Title 18 of the United States Code was amended by adding paragraph (3) g to include as a crime that can be investigated by wiretap:

> "a violation of Section 5322 of Title 31, United States Code (dealing with reporting on currency transactions)."

This extends the area of Fourth Amendment search and seizure violations the government is granted by Congress to invasions of privacy through wire taps. And, in the same group of amendments, the various circumstances under which wiretaps can be implemented without a due diligence order are expanded.

Again, the verbiage does not in any way connect the power of government to wire tap, with regard to currency transactions, to the commission or investigation of any other crimes. With all due respect to the rhetoric that these provisions are aimed at drug traffickers or organized crime, the actual verbiage belies that claim. It is personal financial privacy that is under attack here, by a government that is willing to destroy the Bill of Rights to achieve the end of forcing all of its citizens to make complete revelations of their financial affairs.

This chapter is a bit shorter than the previous three because there has been little definitive case law involving these new provisions. To say the least, there is much in the Comprehensive Crime Control Act of 1984 that suggests a more apt name might be the "People Control Act of 1984."

Chapter 6

The Awesome Power of the IRS

For much of the information covered in this chapter, the author is indebted to the fine work done by Professor Henry M. Holzer and Erika Holzer in their now discontinued newsletter, THE SEC. 7201 REPORT ON TAX EVASION.

In this chapter a few of the many areas that should be of concern to all who fear the erosion of constitutional rights and personal liberty in the United States will be examined. Nowhere has Congress granted greater powers to act in violation of the Bill of Rights than in the portions of the U.S. Code dealing with Internal Revenue. The areas to be dealt with here are:

1. The administrative summons, 26 U.S. Code Sec 7602
2. Perjury as a weapon of the IRS
3. Tax Protesters - non filers.

The administration summons is the first of these powers. How do the courts feel about the IRS Summons? In U.S. vs. Arthur Young & Co., (104 S. CT. 1495, 1984), a case in which the IRS issued a summons for a corporation's tax accrual papers held by Arthur Young and Co., the court in reference to the validity of the summons itself said, "In order to encourage effective tax investigations,

Congress has endowed the IRS with expansive information gathering authority; Section 7602 is the centerpiece of that congressional design . . . and . . . restrictions upon the IRS summons power should be avoided absent unambiguous directions from Congress . . ."

In short, the IRS needs the power to obtain records, Congress has given them that authority, and the Courts have upheld it in its broadest terms. So, in Sec. 7602 this power is granted. What kind of purposes can it be used for? The courts have held that the inclusion of the phrase, "other data" in the Act, means that virtually anything the IRS wants to examine, including handwriting samples, can be obtained through the use of the administrative summons.

Once the IRS has prepared the summons, it goes to federal court with a petition for enforcement under 26 USC Sec. 7604. The government does not have to show very much evidence to get the petition approved. It is required to demonstrate the following:

1. The investigation will be conducted pursuant to a legitimate purpose.

2. The inquiry will be relevant to that purpose.

3. The information sought is not already within the Commissioner's possession and

4. The administrative steps required by the Code have been followed--in essence, that the Secretary has determined further investigation is necessary and has notified the taxpayer in writing to that effect.

This is easily proven through affidavits from the agents involved in the investigation. Prior to TEFRA, if the summons was issued on a third party, the taxpayer merely had to file an objection with the person summoned, instructing him not to comply. At that point, the burden of proof shifted to the government to show cause before the summoned person could be compelled to produce the information, testimony or documents.

Since TEFRA went into effect, the process has been reversed. The burden of proof has now shifted to the taxpayer. He must go to court within 20 days and prove wrongful conduct on the part of the government. The proof must be specific and not merely alleged bad faith. Since, as was stated above, the government need only show in its request a prima facie case, it merely has to reintroduce the same affidavits. Bad faith must be proven, which is almost impossible, even if true.

All of the various tools that the IRS has in its arsenal create multiple opportunities for them to "get" their target. And, if all else fails, they have the tool of perjury--at two levels. Since perjury can happen only when testifying, either under compulsion or voluntarily, using either written or oral material, one is in jeopardy from the moment one has any contact with an agent. In fact, one risks perjury each time a tax return is signed.

There are actually four statutes under which a criminal prosecution can be instituted. The misdemeanor provision is Sec. 7207 of the Internal Revenue Code. The felony provisions are Sec. 7206(1) of the Internal Revenue Code, Sec. 1621 of 18 United States Code, and Sec. 1001 of the United States Code. The latter two do not require a tax liability to be used. Sec. 1001 is the most insidious of these, as shall be seen, but first it is important to review the basics of each.

> SEC. 7207:
>
> To willfully deliver or disclose to the IRS any list, return, account, statement or other document known by the taxpayer to be fraudulent or to be false as to any material matter, shall be fined not more than $1,000 or imprisoned not more than one year or both.
>
> SEC. 7206 (1):
>
> To willfully make and subscribe any return, statement or other document which contains or is verified by a written declaration that is made under the penalties of perjury, and which the taxpayer does not believe to be true and correct as to every material matter, shall be guilty of a felony and, upon conviction thereof, shall be fined not more than $5,000, or imprisoned not more than 3 years or both, together with the costs of prosecution.
>
> SEC. 1621:
>
> To take an oath before any competent tribunal, officer, or person in any case where the law authorizes an oath to be administered, that he will tell the truth or any written testimony, deposition or certificate subscribed is true, willfully and contrary to such oath states or subscribes any material matter which he does not believe

> to be true or (2) in any declaration, certification, verification or statement under penalty of paying as permitted in Sec. 1746 of title 28, United States Code, willfully subscribes as true any material matter which he does not believe to be true is guilty of perjury and shall be fined no more than $2,000 or imprisoned not more than 5 years or both.
>
> SEC. 1001:
>
> To knowingly and willfully make any false statements on any matter within the jurisdiction of any department or agency of the United States shall carry a fine of not more than $10,000 or imprisonment of not more than 5 years or both.

Since 7206 (1) requires a false written declaration and 1621 requires that the perjury be committed under oath, and 1001 merely requires a false statement be made to a federal officer, almost any tax prosecution will also carry with it the additional charges of perjury under 1001.

In U.S. vs. Schonoher, 564 F. 2nd 289 (9th Cir. 1977) the court upheld a 1001 conviction in a tax prosecution, though it called the use of the statute a "draconian course." The judge stated, "This exercise of prosecutorial discretion in this case adds no luster to the concept of government fairness, but the court is forbidden to intervene when the choice of charges is legally committed to the prosecutor."

There is no requirement of materiality in 1001. Any false statement or document given to a federal officer in an inquiry, even though it has nothing to do with liability or the case at hand, can bring on a 1001 prosecution and probably conviction.

Once a false tax return has been filed, the taxpayer can be prosecuted for multiple crimes: 7201 tax evasion, 7206 (1) tax perjury, 1621 general perjury and 1001. The court has even gone so far as to allow 7206 (1) conviction where there was absolutely no tax liability. Merely answering "no" on the 1040 form question about owning a foreign bank account, if untrue, constitutes 7206 (1) perjury even if the account were set up with after-tax funds and had no tax liability.

What is worse, this 1001 conviction takes the case away from evasion and creates the elements of fraud. Fraud is a crime in most countries and therefore helps force tax treaty countries such as Switzerland to open up bank records to the U.S. authorities.

In his November, 1983 issue, Professor Holzer said this about 1001:

> "In sum, once there has been an affirmative, willful, material false statement to the IRS, 1001 has been violated, and, usually there is no defense.
>
> "Recognizing this fact underscores what is probably the most important point of all about 1001: of all the many federal tax crimes, there is less reason to violate 1001 than any other. Why? Because all a taxpayer has to do is remain silent with the IRS agent, resisting any

> temptation to explain, convince, deny, assure, persuade. Remember this: only those people who have made any kind of a statement have been convicted of violating 1001. Thus the ultimate defense is: NEVER TALK TO GOVERNMENT AGENTS EXCEPT THROUGH A QUALIFIED LAWYER."

The next area to be considered will be the IRS's power against tax protesters. There are several million of them out there, which is probably why the bulk of them go unapprehended for years or forever. The IRS just does not have the personnel, nor is there probably room in all of the jails in the U.S. to accommodate every tax protester if the IRS could somehow effectively locate and prosecute all of them. Tax protesters are lumped together as non-filers and those who file frivolous returns.

To begin this section, one must look at Sec. 7203 of the Internal Revenue Code. Whether a tax is owed or not, virtually all citizens are required to file a return and keep records, and when requested, to supply information to IRS. Those who fail to pay a required tax, to file a return, to keep such records or supply information when required are guilty of a crime.

So, simply failing to file a tax return, if required by law, is a crime. Every year that a tax return is not filed is another crime. Moreover, in this day and age, who can really claim ignorance of the law, as an excuse for non-filing. Even the unintentional act is deemed willful.

Therefore, many tax protestors, to avoid a prosecution under 7203 for non-filing, will file with only their names and addresses and everything else left blank or filled with zeros or objections to the law or Fifth Amendment claims. But this will not help. IRS regulations, back by the courts, state that "A taxpayer's return, which does not contain any information from which the tax can be computed, is not a return . . ."

About 15,000 to 18,000 of this class of return are audited each year. And each taxpayer involved can be subject to a 7203 criminal prosecution at the discretion of the IRS. Are there any valid defenses?

TEFRA in 1982 added a $500 civil penalty under Sec. 6702 for filing a frivolous tax return. This should be quoted in its entirety:

> "Sec. 6702 - Frivolous Income Tax Return (a) Civil Penalty. If . . .
>
> (1) any individual files what purports to be a return of tax by subtitle A, but which:
>
> (A) does not contain information on which assessment may be judged, or
>
> (2) the conduct referred to in paragraph (1) is due to:
>
> (A) a position which is frivolous, or
>
> (B) a desire (which appears on the purported return) to delay or impede the administration of federal income tax laws, then such

> individaul shall pay a penalty of $500."

Two recent classic cases under 6702 were Miller vs. U.S. 577 7. Supp. 980 (USDC N.D. Indiana, 1984) and Tibbets vs. Secretary of the Treasury 577 7. Supp. 911 (USDC W.D. North Carolina, 1984). In Tibbets the court found that, "Congress' purpose in providing for an immediately accessible civil penalty for frivolous income tax returns was to deter the filing of protest returns ..."

This includes, in the long list of cases, questioning wages being income, legal tender, the legality of the income tax, using the Fifth Amendment or leaving questions blank or attaching tax protest literature.

Since nothing need be proven except the act itself, this is an almost unbeatable weapon in the IRS' arsenal against tax protestors. But even worse, once the court has ruled on the civil violation, this opens up the door to criminal action, as there is a subsection at the end of 6702, which states that "The penalty imposed by subsection (2) shall be in addition to any other penalty provided by law."

Remember, the courts have consistently held that an incomplete return is not a return at all. Thus, once the court has imposed the civil fine, the IRS can then institute a criminal 7203 action for failure to file. This also provides the elements, if any tax is owing, as is the case in most tax protest returns, for a 7201 tax evasion prosecution.

So, to be a tax protester makes the individual an easy target. The weapons that the IRS can use against the everyday taxpayer, who fudges a little here and there, are awesome but these pale before the gargantuan power that the IRS can mobilize against tax protesters who open themselves up to special scrutiny. In fact, the only real protection that protesters have is their sheer numbers. As a result, many will slip through the net merely because of the lack of IRS personnel or sufficient jail space.

This has been a peek at the awesome power of the IRS. There is much, much more. Clearly, the intent of the Founding Fathers to create a society of free men has come into conflict with the IRS. Unfortunately, Congress and the court system have opted to remove constitutional guarantees in favor of virtually unlimited power in the hands of IRS.

Chapter 7

The Domestic Privacy Scene

A profound and frightening change has come over the U.S. financial scene since early 1985. As part of the U.S. government attack on drug traffic, the currency transaction reporting requirement (over $10,000) law is being enforced--and broadened--like never before. It is clearly the bureaucrats' intent to make banks, brokerage houses, and even coin dealers report all large cash transactions. Moreover, even specific employees of these institutions are being targeted. Because of the activities of drug dealers, casino operators, and other "businesses" dealing in cash, the financial freedoms of all Americans are under savage attack.

About two years ago, the IRS decided to go after U.S. banks not reporting large cash transactions. Since that time, many large banks, from Bank of America on down, have been hit with multi-million dollar fines. These fines have been so stiff that now banks are bending over backwards to comply, indeed, to over-comply, with reporting regulations. The problem now facing the IRS is too many records being sent from the banks, some of which, to protect themselves, have even started to report certain cash transactions below $10,000.

Every week now brings new horror stories of the courts and regulators cracking down. For instance--as this book is being written--two landmark incidents have occurred. These incidents illustrate graphically the new climate facing the financial industry.

The Bank Secrecy Act of 1970 was directed against financial institutions. This was always taken to mean banks. But after successfully cowing the banks into compliance the feds are going after a hitherto untouched group: the brokerage houses. In late June, 1986, Shearson Lehman Brothers was indicted by a federal grand jury on charges of laundering $1.2 million in illegal gambling money into legitimate investments. The firm is accused of changing the undeclared cash first into unreportable money orders and bank checks and then using these new Shearson accounts to buy tax-free municipal bonds. If convicted, both the firm and the alleged broker face maximum fines of $16 million apiece! In addition, the broker faces a 198-year prison term. This action against a specific individual broker is also unprecedented. The 1970 act, to repeat, was directed against financial institutions and not individuals. So, there was some question as to whether the government could lock up a broker for life. But one day after the Shearson indictment, a Federal appeals court

(Second Circuit) decided in a related case that a brokerage house employee could be convicted of criminal charges for causing his firm to violate the reporting transaction requirements. In this case, a former broker for Merrill Lynch was accused. Unlike the Shearson case, the government did not believe the firm itself was involved, only the broker. The case involved a married couple, the Silbers, who brought a large cash deposit to the broker, Alan Heyman, who, in order to avoid the $10,000 CTR, divided the sum into several accounts in names of Silber family members. Even though "Heyman himself had no legal responsibility to file Currency Transaction Reports" said Judge Irving Kaufman--only institutions do--"by structuring his customers' deposits so that no single transaction involved an amount greater than $10,000, Heyman caused Merrill Lynch to fail to file the appropriate CTR. Had Merrill Lynch, a financial institution, structured the transactions the way Heyman did, it would have violated Federal law. [Therefore] Heyman is criminally liable." His sentence was relatively light three years of probation.

After this case, no broker would be expected to aid someone who wanted to break down a large amount into sums below $10,000.

Given the unfriendly new environment born of the past few months, it would be untruthful for anyone to tell you that there are many ways left to protect your financial privacy. There aren't. Perhaps in a few years Americans will become fed up enough with the relentless attacks on their privacy to demand changes. But, for now, the list of viable methods is short.

Or, perhaps more correctly, the list of viable and SIMPLE methods is short. Any choice should be a simple one. There are stories of new identities and passports, but these methods become so tangled that, unless one is a professional money launderer, it is easy to slip up. Besides, one wonders if the whole exercise is worth the trouble.

Indeed, there are good arguments for the position that if an individual is an American, one should choose a safe haven like Switzerland or Austria and simply declare everything when opening an account there. No one knows what is going to happen in the future, and many people keep money overseas for fear of exchange controls. However, a number of experts believe it very unlikely that a future U.S. government, even if it passed exchange control laws, would require its citizens to repatriate the money already overseas. More likely, the new laws would only apply to those who are still trying to move money out of the country. Viewed from this perspective, a foreign bank account becomes a valuable tool for taking advantage of special international investments, a part of a diversified portfolio, money socked away from ex-wives or relatives, a savings account whose contents are a bit more difficult to spend. Thus, the question of using a foreign bank account to evade taxes does not enter into the equation.

There is much to be said for this attitude, particularly in a climate where the U.S. government's new strategy seems to be (1) lower tax rates and, (2) go after those not paying what they owe. Certainly, for many people, a foreign bank account, openly declared, would allow them to sleep better at night.

Those intent on building up wealth unknown to anyone can still do so. But, in general, they will have to spend a relatively large part of their time making relatively small amounts private. Of course, small amounts can add up. Here are some of the things one can do legally.

In this section, only transactions taking place within North America will be discussed. Overseas transactions will be covered in Chapter 8.

BUYING COINS

Coins are still one of the best ways to enhance privacy. Listed below are several tips one can use to keep purchase--and storage--transactions completely private.

Thus, to escape any reporting requirements on coins, one can:

1. Use the same coin dealer, spreading (under

$10,000) purchases out over time--at least a few weeks between transactions.

2. Buy and sell coins at coin shows. These are attended primarily by dealers, not retail customers. Thus dealers assume that those in attendance are fellow coin dealers. Dealer-to-dealer trades are not reportable, nor are local sales taxes imposed in most cases.

3. Buy and sell coins privately. If one attends hard money seminars, or knows hard money investors locally, it might pay to consider establishing buying and selling arrangements between oneself and like-minded private investors. It's probable that coin trading in the classified ads will expand rapidly over the next few years.

Storing metal within the U.S. can also be done privately. The idea here is to arrange things so one doesn't have to give a tax-payer I.D. number (Social Security number) when opening a safe-deposit box. As is common knowledge, one must give this number at all U.S. banks. This type of box is what most people think of when they consider metals storage. There are, however, private, non-bank deposit box depositories. These non-bank deposit boxes, as well as other methods: home storeage; commodity exchange warehouses; and Canadian safe-deposit boxes, will now be explored.

HOME STORAGE

Everyone should have some coins at home where they will be easily accessible in an emergency. Here are some ideas on in-home storage that do not require professional help.

One may, of course, want professional help, but in order to ensure complete secrecy, nobody outside of one's immediate family should know about the hiding place. It may be possible to find an honest contractor who's done enough of this type of work that one more job will be meaningless, forgotten as soon as it's finished. But there is no way to be certain. And, obviously, it's a plain contradiction to have a secret hiding place that someone else knows about. Aside of the secrecy considerations, there is another reason to construct an in-home storage area oneself: the thrill of creating something so useful can be a real morale builder.

Note: There is no such thing as 100% safety. If an intruder is smart enough, and is willing to take enough time, he can rip one's house or apartment apart and find whatever is hidden. The purpose of a secret hiding place is simply to make it more difficult for any thief--hopefully so hard that he will go away empty handed.

Of course, the owner must always remember where valuables are stored. One man stored coins in a drain pipe, forgot about this, and then got cleaned out after a visit by the plumbers.

USING YOUR BOOKS

A bookcase can be a good place to hide valuables. The simplest (and also least safe) way is the hollow book. This method works best for the person who has plenty of books for a burglar to search through. Unfortunately, these fake books often look fake. This problem can be solved by fitting a jacket from a real book over the imitation one. A criminal willing to take the time can still find the fake, but it means more work.

A far more secure method, which also gives one more hiding space, involves using the bottom shelf of one's bookcase. Usually the lowest shelf, raised at least three inches from the floor, juts out over a baseboard which hides the empty space. To make this space accessible, one makes the bottom shelf removable.

The easiest way is to have the bottom shelf simply resting on the baseboard. It's an easy matter to remove the books on the bottom shelf to get to one's valuables.

But, as a general rule, the easier it is for the owner to get to his coins, the easier it is for a burglar. A more secure elaboration on the same idea is this: there are nails or plugs from the outside planks that hold the bottom shelf firm. Normally, narrow headed "finishing" nails are used for this purpose, and anyone looking at the nails flush up against the wood would think them immovable.

Here is how one can deceive an intruder. If holes, slightly larger than the nails, are drilled with an electric drill, and nails are pushed through by hand, these then can be removed with a magnet. In fact, the use of magnets on nails is bounded only by one's imagination. (Strong magnets are available from your local hardware store; Edmund Scientific sells a 3.5 pound war-surplus magnet that can lift 40 pounds. Write them for a free catalog at 300 Edscorp Building, Barrington, New Jersey 08007.)

Of course, this is more easily done on a bookcase that one actually builds. Otherwise it may be necessary to strip and refinish the entire case to disguise one's work.

SPICY STORAGE

The spice rack in one's kitchen can also be used as a hiding place. The only provision is that it have a back, which will serve as the door to a secret compartment. Trace the outline of the back of the spice rack on the wall with a pencil, then carve a hole in the wall using a drill, hammer and chisel, or keyhole saw. The only limitation on this type of storage area is the depth and makeup of the wall itself.

Be sure to leave a border of an inch or so around the hole where the false nails can go on to hold up the rack. A classier version involves false bolts. The idea is to convince a thief, if one were to ever look, that the rack, attached with bolts and washers, is an immovable structure. In reality, though, the bolts have been cut through by a hacksaw and pounded in only a little way.

What actually holds up the rack are the fastener snaps. All hardware stores carry these common friction holders. One side is attached to the back of the rack, the other to the approximately one inch border surrounding the hole. At least two fasteners will be necessary, but use as many as desired. The more snaps, the harder the yank required to separate the rack from the wall.

Magnet snaps can also be used. These are not nearly as strong as friction snaps, but if enough are used, one gets the same effect.

All of these techniques involving false nails, false bolts, magnets and other fasteners can be employed using other household fixtures as well to create secret storage places.

BASE TECHNIQUES

One of the best places to hide things is behind the baseboards that run around every room in one's house or apartment. In older dwellings, these tend to be taller, which gives one even more space.

1. Check around the house, including closets, for lengths of baseboard that can easily be removed. Look to see where one length of baseboard meets another at a corner, or abuts a door jamb. There will be an almost invisible crack here. However, for this purpose, it's better if such cracks can be seen. When making a movable baseboard, the fact that its crack is slightly more evident than others will not attract the wrong kind of attention.

2. Working slowly and carefully, pry the length of baseboard from the wall. Don't damage the baseboard or the wall. In the likely event that the board doesn't move under hand pressure, use a thin-bladed screwdriver. A crowbar will increase the chance of damage.

If it is impossible to avoid some damage, one may have to repaint the entire board. If the paint can't be matched exactly, and the boards are painted the same color as the room, it may be necessary to repaint everything. A different-color baseboard will, of course, result in exactly what one wants to avoid: an attention-getter.

Redoing the baseboard in one or more rooms of an old house can be a great decorating idea. Stripping off all the old paint and refinishing them leaves a beautiful wood grain, as well as plenty of joining cracks for one's purpose.

3. Once the board is off and the area behind laid bare, one may find space already available. The builders, knowing that there would be baseboard covering that portion of the wall, may have left it only partially plastered. But, chances are that it will be solid plasterboard or a wooden wall. Choosing one's tools--hammer and chisel or drill or keyhole saw--create the needed space.

The best way to rejoin the baseboard to the wall is snap or magnetic fasteners. To minimize damage when removing the board, place the fasteners close to an indentation or hole, where an inserted finger or screwdriver won't cause damage. The magnet-to-nail idea can also be used, as can Velcro strips.

THE ELECTRIC PLUG RUSE

One can also pick a seldom-used electrical outlet and turn it into a storage area for coins.

1. Make sure the main electrical switch is off before doing anything to an outlet.

2. Using a screwdriver, remove the exterior face plate and disconnect all electrical wires by unscrewing the leads. Cover each piece of base wire with heavy electrician's tape and push or bend the wires out of the way to create space.

3. Choose the method of attachment one wants to use. If more space is required, remove the metal electrical box

inside. This will also remove the holes for the screws, so use magnetic or Velcro fasteners.

BACKYARD STORAGE

For metals buried in one's back-yard, there is a modern variation on treasure chests. One of the most popular methods of home storage has been the so called "Midnight-Gardener." These are three plastic capsules of varying sizes.

The smallest (2" x 12") can hold 100 one-ounce gold coins; the largest (6" x 12") can hold a bag of $1,000 face value silver coins. The middle capsule measures 4" x 12", and holds a half bag of silver coins.

They are made of extruded PVC (polyvinylchloride). This same material is used in underground water and sewage systems because it is resistant to all elements found in the soil, including water and chemicals. The capsules are also explosion resistant, capable of withstanding the stress of 200 pounds per square inch.

The Midnight Gardener was developed by Investment Rarities, the coin dealer. To protect the privacy of all capsule purchasers, it destroys the records of client names and addresses immediately after shipment.

IRI charges $39 for the 1-bag capsule, $24.95 for the 1/2 bag capsule, and $12.95 for the 100 gold coin capsule. But, IRI officials point out that one can probably make one's own capsule much more cheaply. Building and plumbing supply companies stock large amounts of extruded PVC. Some companies will cut a piece off the pipe, and sell you the end caps as well.

If, however, one doesn't want to construct the capsules, they are available from IRI, One Appletree Square, Minneapolis MN 55420. (Minn. residents add 4% sales tax.)

Of course, there are also drawbacks to the Midnight Gardener. The existence of buried pirate treasure lost for centuries should alert anyone to the fact that there are some obvious disadvantages to this method:

* One could forget where it is buried.

* One could die without the heirs knowing the treasure's location

* One is vulnerable to any person who, armed with a metal detector, gains entry to the area where the capsule is buried. Of course, it's illegal to trespass on someone's property with a metal detector, but thieves out to steal one's gold won't be deterred by that fact.

* If one has 20 coins and wants to sell only 5 of them, it's a big problem.

HOME STORAGE SUMMATION

In summary, like everything else, it's up to each person to decide if the drawbacks outweigh the benefits.

Pros: Metals are under your most direct control.

Cons: Vulnerable to thieves, one's own forgetfulness, or loose lips.

PRIVATE SAFETY DEPOSIT BOXES

This became a growth industry in the early 1980s. Perhaps over 200 companies have been started since 1979. However, the failure rate for new companies has been very high as well. About half of these have already gone under. Some of these bankruptcies left the box holders unaware, without enough time to claim their boxes before they were opened by the bankruptcy courts.

So far, though, there has been no clear-cut case of the private vault owner absconding with the assets entrusted to him. It could happen, of course, especially with the scores of new entrants in the field. Much more likely, however, given the high mortality rate in this business--is that the vault company itself would go out of business. It would then be necessary to find another place for one's valuables.

It is obviously better to do business with a vault company that won't go bankrupt: one that will "beat the odds" and still be in business three years from now. To this end, a set of questions has been developed that should be put to any potential warehouser of one's metals. (Much of this information has been taken from Chris Weber's

Complete Guide to Safe Storage of Silver & Gold, $68 to DRA Publishing Co, 251 Lafayette Circle, Lafayette CA 94549).

Some of these questions should concern every potential client: they provide clues as to whether or not the company will be here tomorrow. Others deal with questions of privacy and access. Some people will be more interested in these than others.

HOW LONG HAVE YOU BEEN IN BUSINESS?

As with any industry, a business that has been operating for 10 years has a much better chance of being around for 10 more than does a company that has only been open for 2 years. Of the thousands of new businesses started each year, most won't last a decade. Ten years is a good rule of thumb. A company started in 1974 will have lasted two recessions. One could even apply a stricter standard.

As of year-end 1983, there were about 4.5 million businesses in the U.S. Not even 2% of these were in business in 1933, 50 years earlier.

And yet, there still exist a handful of private vaults that were in business a half-century ago. These include exchange warehouses, as well as private safe-deposit boxes. For instance, Day and Night Safe Deposit of Seattle was founded in 1909.

Clearly, private metals storage is a growth industry. It's attracted hundreds of entrepreneurs in the past three years. Obviously, some of these are going to survive. The best will have used new technology to become more secure and will be set up to cater to the needs of modern metals storers. So don't cross a company off your list because it just opened its doors.

WHAT ARE YOUR HOURS?

Some people want 24-hour access because they fear bank holidays. Others have jobs during banking hours. The rule is that, while private vaults usually offer liberal hours of access, the so-called exchange warehouses keep banker's hours.

WHAT DID THE OWNERS DO PRIOR TO GETTING INTO THE VAULT BUSINESS?

When entrusting metals to a storer, one generally feels the safest knowing that the owner has long experience in the precious metals industry. This is a new industry and people generally come to it from other areas. Most private vault owners have construction or real estate backgrounds.

WHO BUILT YOUR VAULT?

Usually, it's better when a recognized vault builder, such as Mosler or Diebold, built the vault door. When the vault owners say that they built the vault themselves, or that it was done by a local contractor, or that they've used bits from several companies, it could mean that they skimped on the vault construction.

But there are very, very few storage firms designed and built by people who understand hard-money and whose facilities are expressly built for the private individual storage of precious metals and other hard assets. However, these few firms are quite familiar with the recent spotty history of certain coin dealers, know that metals investors tend to want privacy, and have responded well to the needs of their clients.

Furthermore, they know the dangers involved when dealers of metals also offer to store the commodity. Hence, they only store.

One example of a firm run with the metals investor in mind is Guardian Safe Deposit of Arlington, Virginia. It was founded by two long-time employees of Deak-Perera, one of whom was responsible for setting up Deak's metals certificate program.

ASK FOR REFERENCES, AUDITS, AND FINANCIAL STATEMENTS

Always obtain the names, official titles, addresses and phone numbers of the firm's bankers. No honest businessman should object to giving bank references.

These will tell the metals owner if the firm pays its bills on time and may give one insight into the way it does business. Unfortunately, some of the questions one might ask prospective coin dealers don't apply to most storers. For instance, it would clearly help to see a firm's financial statement before entrusting one's valuables to it. Similarly, it would be good to know if the firm has been audited by an independent body.

Unfortunately, virtually all safe-deposit companies are privately held. Owners will usually not give out any balance sheet information for their companies because these reveal, at least in part, the owners' net worths. These owners take the position that it is no one's business what they control or own.

This is one area where the exchange warehouses (examined next), offer an advantage. Because banks are regulated, they must make available their internal financial information. However, even the fanciest audit statement in the world won't, in and of itself, guarantee the financial viability of a company.

DO THEY OFFER CONFIDENTIALITY?

Confidentiality is a prime reason for using private vaults. Of course, most companies offer it, but not all. Be sure to check. At most private vaults, one's identity is secret; they have no idea who their customers are.

Perhaps, only one's number and, maybe, a password are known. Be sure not to spoil this anonymity by paying a storage bill with a traceable check.

Chris Weber surveyed nearly 100 private storers and, in the end recommended only 11. Here are a few of these:

1. Day & Night Safe Deposit & Storage
   507 Third Avenue
   Seattle, WA 98104
   (206) 622-0722

2. Guardian Safe Deposit
   2499 N. Harrison Street
   Arlington, VA 22207
   (703) 237-1133

3. Security Center
   147 Carondelet Street
   New Orleans, LA 70130
   (504) 522-1254

4. Universal Safe Deposit Corp.
   115 East 57th Street
   New York, NY 10022
   (212) 644-0124

Additional private vault references can be found in the final chapter.

NOTE ON PRIVATE STORERS

Be sure to get insurance through a separate entity. Many policies exist that pay off specifically to the metals owner, in the event of fraud. Any of the companies listed above should be able to steer one to a competent broker. (Guardian certainly can). For a complete survey, get the Weber book.

SUMMATION

Pros: A storer can store metals, diamonds, or any valuables in one's own box with confidentiality and round-the-clock accessibility.

Cons: There may be no reputable facilities in an area. Also, a separate insurance policy is a must.

EXCHANGE WAREHOUSES

What one calls "exchange warehouses" are the certified warehouses where banks, brokerage houses, metals dealers, and commodity exchanges store THEIR silver and gold. These are warehouses where metals are stacked together rather than being separated into individual piles, in most cases.

Before having read Weber's book, the author assumed that Comex and other institutions stored their metals in vaults which were closed to individual investors, or at least those with assets below the Bunker Hunt level. Happily, he discovered that any vault which stores metals for large institutions will also store for small investors. Curiously, no one had ever seen mention made of this opportunity.

The advantages of taking this route are obvious. There are probably few places as safe as these to store one's metals--safe not only from thieves, but from bankruptcy as well.

Even though many of these exchange warehouses are banks, the stored metals are not considered deposits of the banks. There is therefore no debtor-creditor relationship. Rather, the relationship is that of a "bailor-bailee." This means that one has hired the bank to store one's metals, but title to them belongs clearly to the owner. So, if proper procedures have been followed by the bank, these metals are beyond the grasp of the bank creditors, should insolvency occur.

If the bank were to become insolvent, it would be taken over by the FDIC. No one has ever heard of an exchange warehouse becoming insolvent, so there is no way to know how easy it would be to reclaim one's metals from an FDIC-administered bank. But judging from what the FDIC does to stop safe-deposit boxholders from retrieving their belongings from normal insolvent banks--nothing--it would seem most unlikely that there would be any withdrawal problems at a bankrupt exchange warehouse.

This would probably hold true short of a general bank holiday, or a general confiscation of private gold. In the latter case, exchange warehouses would be the first to be hit. But, as discussed earlier, should that ever come to pass, many believe that, this time around, even the private vault companies would be sealed. The only safe places would be at one's home or in a safe jurisdiction overseas.

This brings up a potential drawback of many--but not all--of the exchange warehouses. Unlike private vaults, many warehouses require a social security number to open an account. Paradoxically however, the three warehouses which the author considers the best--Bank of Delaware, Wilmington Trust, and Rhode Island Hospital Trust--only require such identification if one sells the metal, not if it is simply stored. These three firms are the only warehouses that the author has found with such a policy; all the rest require identification. As a result, while the addresses of all exchange warehouses have been included, these three are the only ones that can be recommended.

This is not to say that these warehouses will guarantee complete Swiss-style confidentiality. If the tax man really wants to find out one's identity in this country, he will. But at least one is an additional step removed from snoopers.

Earlier it was mentioned that metals held at these warehouses, or at least those held by private individuals, are stacked together. This means that there are no individual metal box dividers separating each holding. All clients' metals are kept separate from the bank's assets, but only institutional holders, not private individuals, have divided storage areas.

What usually happens is that all of the warehouse's institutional customers have segregated metals holdings, while those of private individuals are stored together. So far, individual holdings make up such a small part (under 5%) of most warehouses' inventories that this method of storage has been the rule. However, very large individual accounts are also kept separate. But regardless of whether one's coins are actually tagged with serial numbers, when metal is bought, it is stored in the owner's name and audited regularly. If an individual demands to have his metal set aside with his name or number on it, the warehouse may comply. Since so few individuals know about this method of storage, there are as yet too few customers to provide the warehouse with a firm set of practices.

While it is usually important to get one's own insurance when storing metals in private vaults, it is not vital with exchange warehouses. Unlike private or regular bank safe-deposit boxes, there are so many built-in safeguards that one needn't bother with extra insurance, if storing metals at, say, the Bank of Delaware. This particular bank's insurance policy makes the client a direct beneficiary.

There is one clear drawback to exchange warehouses from which there's really no escape. Hours and conditions of access are strictly limited. All of these warehouses keep banker's hours, and only one which Weber contacted, Republic National Bank, indicated that it would be open on weekends, but only for "good" (i.e., large) customers. As to what constitutes "good", no definitive amount was given. However, Weber got the distinct impression that the value of an account would have to be well into six figures for the bank to alter its 9-5 schedule.

Keep in mind that these hours of operation, meager as they may seem compared to those of some private vaults, are for warehouse customers to deposit or withdraw institutional metals, or, more often, for the auditors of institutional clients to visit and inspect metals holdings.

But one thing that is not allowed is for individual owners to come in to "visit" their metals. Keep in mind that the overwhelming majority of exchange warehouse customers are institutions. The Bank of Delaware, for instance, counts individual clients as a mere 3% of total metals stored. The warehouses regard individuals' visits as nuisances. The only way one can expect to see the metals is to pay a withdrawal fee upon closing out the account, or have the warehouse arrange for an armored car delivery. (But as explained below, there is a very easy way to get one's metal back, even though the exact coins are not returned.)

So, as a general rule, if storing at an exchange warehouse, do not expect to actually see the coins stored there. This is usually even true at the outset, when one wants to place the coins in storage.

It is not possible to just walk in off the street with metals and ask the exchange warehouse to store them. At the very least, the metals must be assayed. The charge for this is about $125-$150. Depending on the amount of metals to be stored, there may be a handling charge as well. Some warehouses will not even take the time to assay in-coming metals. They just aren't set-up to handle metals in this way. And the charges levied, by those that will, make this an awkward proposition.

Don't despair though. There is an easier way. Buy metals from an established broker, who, in turn, stores with a particular exchange warehouse. When buying, one merely instructs the dealer to, in effect, transfer the metal from his account at the warehouse to one's own account.

In Weber's view, the best warehouse to use is that of the Bank of Delaware. Quite apart from its other advantages, the bank has the distinction of housing metals for every large metals dealer in the U.S. Mocatta Metals, Merrill Lynch, Shearson/American Express, Deak-Perera, J. Aron, Republic National Bank; all the big names are there.

Inquire to see if a prospective dealer maintains an account at the Bank of Delaware. Merrill Lynch Precious Metals does, for example. Simply ask that the metal one buys be stored in the purchaser's name at the bank. The metal will be separated from the physical Merrill Lynch holdings and moved to the section reserved for individual holdings. There is usually no extra charge for this, no assay fee, no transfer fee. The metal is already at the bank and assayed.

Moreover, if the individual wants to see any part of his holdings, it can be transferred back to Merrill Lynch's Bank of Delaware account, at which time the individual's broker can either give him the coins or write him a check. (Note: Weber used Merrill Lynch as an example; other dealers have similar policies.)

A note about warehouse security. Not surprisingly, all of the warehouses rival the best of the private vaults. (The private Security Center in New Orleans used to be a Federal Reserve Bank). Furthermore, very strict access policies--which effectively close the warehouse off to all but auditors and VIPs--are in place to make the vault even more secure.

The minimum storage amounts are fairly standard, and very reasonable. One can generally store as little as one Krugerrand or half a bag ($500 face value) of silver coins, as well as any size of bullion bar.

The three best warehouses, according to Weber, will be examined in the following section. Listed in alphabetical order, a brief synopsis of each will be given:

BANK OF DELAWARE

The Bank of Delaware is Weber's favorite place to store metals in the U.S., at least those metals that one doesn't plan to see and fondle. In longevity, in breadth of service, in respectability, and last but not least, in plain courtesy, the Bank of Delaware stands out among the other exchange warehouses.

The Bank of Delaware was founded in 1795. It almost certainly stored gold and silver from the start. However, the Bank's niche in storing metals for the country's biggest metal brokers dates only from 1978.

Its premier position has undoubtedly been a result of the fact that Delaware levies no tax on the purchase or storage of metals.

As the largest bank in Delaware, with assets of over $1 billion and a history of uninterrupted dividend payments since 1796, the Bank of Delaware fell quite naturally into the role of Delaware's foremost metals storer.

As mentioned earlier, Merrill Lynch, Shearson/American Express, Republic National Bank, and Deak-Perera are just a few of the giants that use the American Gold Coin Exchange. All this really means is that, if one's regular coin or bullion dealer is large enough to have an account at the Bank, account openings and storage can easily be arranged by transferring metals, already in the bank's vaults, from the coin or bullion dealer's account to that established by the purchasing individual.

VAULTS is the term used because there is too much metal housed at the Bank to fit in a one vault-warehouse. The Bank of Delaware stores as much silver as all the banks in New York City put together. This means that silver is housed in many different electronically-protected areas. Gold, on the other hand, is kept in a single warehouse.

Again, the Bank does not require a Social Security number to open a metals storage account. The easiest way to open such an account is simply to buy metals from a dealer who also stores there and request Bank storage.

Fees are very straightforward, compared to the other warehouses. Annual fees are 1/4% (0.25%) for gold and 1/2% (0.50%) for silver. These are charged at the outset. All fees must be paid in advance and are based on the value at the outset. There is a minimum annual charge of $30.

RHODE ISLAND HOSPITAL TRUST

This warehouse derives its name from the fact that it was started by the state of Rhode Island as an institution to finance a hospital.

Afterward, it became a regular trust company. The warehouse has nothing to do with a hospital, so banish any thoughts of your silver and gold being stored in bed pans.

Since 1968 it has stored metals. One warehouse also acts as a bullion dealer. There are no minimums. Fees are 25 cents per 100 ounces per day for gold; 6 cents per 1,000 ounces per day for silver.

The easiest way to store metals here is to buy them from Brinks and have them transferred into one's account. Most big dealers can also arrange storage at the Rhode Island Hospital.

WILMINGTON TRUST

A recent entry into the ranks of exchange warehouses is the Wilmington Trust. Like the Bank of Delaware, this institution is headquartered in Wilmington, Delaware and, strictly speaking, is not a depository for the commodity exchanges.

While it is one of the larger trust companies in the U.S.--15th, according to a recent report--the Wilmington Trust only got into the individual metals storage industry in late 1984. As of this writing it doesn't have nearly the amount of volume that the Bank of Delaware has, but it gives the impression of being very eager for new business and would, obviously, love to eventually rival the Bank of Delaware. The Wilmington Trust's big advantage is that it already rivals the Bank of Delaware in security, privacy, and insurance.

At present its biggest drawback is that, unlike its larger neighbor, the Wilmington Trust has no retail metals dealers as clients. As such, individuals cannot buy coins at a local dealer and then have them transferred from the dealer's account in the warehouse to the individual's own account. However, it seems only a matter of time before the Wilmington Trust has rectified this problem.

ADDRESSES FOR RECOMMENDED WAREHOUSES

1. Bank of Delaware
519 N. Market
Wilmington, DL 19899
(302) 429-1210

2. Wilmington Trust Co.
Rodney Square North
Wilmington, DL 19890
(302) 651-1000

3. Rhode Island Hospital
1 Hospital Trust Plaza
Providence, RI 02903
(401) 278-8174

OTHER WAREHOUSES

1. Chase Manhattan Bank
One Chase Manhattan Plaza
New York, NY 10015
(212) 552-0850

2. Citibank
399 Park Avenue
New York, NY 10043
(212) 559-7776

3. First National Bank of Chicago
   1 First National Plaza
   Chicago, IL 60670
   (312) 732-4000

4. Continental Illinois Bank
   231 S. LaSalle
   Chicago, IL 60697
   (312) 828-2345

5. Harris Bank & Trust
   P.O. Box 755
   Chicago, IL 60690
   (312) 461-2121

6. Irving Trust Company
   One Wall Street
   New York, NY 10015
   (212) 487-2231

7. Swiss Bank Corporation
   4 World Trade Center
   New York, NY 10048
   (212) 938-3500

8. Republic National Bank
   450 Fifth Avenue
   New York, NY 10018
   (212) 930-6000

9. Iron Mountain Depository
   26 Broadway
   New York, NY 10004
   (212) 938-9696

SUMMATION

Pros: Warehouses provide confidentiality and probably the safest storage in the U.S.

Cons: Exchange warehouses are only for metals, not for diamonds, stocks, etc. Also, these metals are not easily accessible to the average investor.

A LOOK AT CANADIAN BANKS

Thusfar in this chapter, only private metals storage in the U.S. has been explored. However, it is worth taking a look at Canadian banks, which are not quite the same as our banks in the U.S.

The biggest differences between Canadian and U.S. banks is that one isn't required to give identification, such as a Social Security number, to rent a safe-deposit box in Canada. Usually all that is necessary is a driver's license. Sometimes a second I.D. may be required, e.g., a passport.

Canadian banking law follows the British tradition of confidentiality. This is nothing like the Swiss secrecy. But, Americans are often surprised to find out that, in some areas, the Commonwealth tradition respects privacy more than does American law.

One still needs a taxpayer I.D. to open a Canadian CHECKING account. And foreign bank accounts need to be reported to the IRS. But safe-deposit boxes do not fall under this requirement.

If one doesn't want to open an account at the bank, debiting it to pay the annual box fees, there are several alternatives. One of these is to have the bank bill one's home address. Banks do require a billing address. A second alternative is to pay a few years in advance. A third is simply to pay when one visits the bank--a very private method indeed. As is the method of mailing in a money order when billed. (Incidentally, most banks send out billings in January or February, not the best time to visit the frozen north).

The sums involved are not large. They are low enough to allow one to use an anonymous money order (those which don't require I.D.'s to buy). Prices of the various sized boxes, offered by the Bank of Nova Scotia (BONS), are given below. This bank is a leading precious metals dealer. In addition, most of its offices are open from 10AM-3PM on Saturday, as well as during regular banking hours--10AM-4PM Monday/Thursday and 10AM-6PM on Friday.

BONS Safe-Deposit Box Prices
as of July, 1984

1 1/2 x 5 x 24 inches	$18
2 1/2 x 5 x 24 inches	$25
2 1/2 x 10 3/4 x 24 inches	$40
5 x 10 3/8 x 24 inches	$75
10 x 10 3/4 x 24 inches	$143

Remember, all figures are in Canadian dollars. At current exchange rates, reduce them by one-quarter to get corresponding U.S. prices.

BONS prices are representative of all the Canadian banks. Since the prices of the two others checked--Canadian Imperial Bank of Commerce and the Bank of British

Columbia--were exactly the same sized boxes, it is probable that all banks move in lockstep, at least in price. BONS was the only bank surveyed that offered Saturday openings. But, paradoxically, don't expect the main headquarters in a large Canadian financial center to be open on Saturday. Financial districts are deserted on the weekends. Saturday openings apply only to neighborhoods where people live.

In addition to banks in Canada, there are trusts. Trusts operate under restrictions to which banks are not subject. For instance, trusts can't make commercial loans. But with regard to safe-deposit boxes, banks and trusts are the same. Trust's prices, if anything, tend to be a bit lower than those of banks. Here are the prices of a representative Canadian trust:

GUARANTY TRUST

2 x 5 x 20 inches	$15
5 x 3 x 20 inches	$20
5 x 5 x 20 inches	$30

As one can see, while the smallest BONS box is 180 cubic inches and rents for $18 (U.S. $13.50), Guaranty's smallest box is a larger 200 cubic inches and rents for $15 (U.S. $11.25). Quite a lot can fit in such a box. A box of 200 cubic inches will easily hold 300 Krugerrands, worth at today's prices over $100,000 (U.S.$). That's not bad for $11 per year. The Canadian government does not insure deposit boxes. As with institutions in the U.S., one needs to purchase insurance separately.

Guardian Trust is a major Canadian metals dealer that also offers a storage program. This is segregated safe-keeping in its vault, rather than individual deposit boxes. All metal is kept in one warehouse, but segregated by name.

Guardian Trust charges 1/4% (0.25%) of total value, figured on the last day of the year. There is a $50 (Canadian $) minimum. It is obvious that this method is far more expensive than that of owning one's own box. The small Guaranty Trust box, which can fit $100,000 (U.S.$) worth of bullion coins, costs $11 (U.S. B.$) per year. The same 300 Krugerrands would cost $262.50 (U.S.$) at Guardian Trust.

In addition, there is a place on the Guardian Trust storage application for your taxpayer I.D. number. A Guardian officer told Weber: "There are no reporting requirements as of yet, but if the laws change we would be obliged to comply."

It is doubtful that, whatever the advantages gained by dealing with Guardian, it is worth the extra price. The storing of some metals in a Guardian box must be seriously considered, though. The combination of privacy, safety and price is hard to beat. The term "safety" is used, not just because one is dealing with banks, but because it is improbable that Canada, a major gold producer, would move to confiscate gold as soon as the U.S. would.

There are no specific banks or trusts in Canada which stand out in service vis-a-vis their safe-deposit boxes. All are about the same. Guardian Trust is the Canadian institution most frequently associated with precious metals. Although the metal is still segregated, it is not kept in individual compartments for each client.

SUMMATION

Pros: Canadian bank or trust storage is confidential and not expensive.

Cons: It may require inconvenient visits.

Chapter 8

Foreign Privacy Havens

Obviously, Canadian banks are not domestic institutions. Rather, the brief discussion of last chapter serves as a percursor to the rest of this book, all of which will be devoted to foreign privacy havens. These havens seem to be the only real alternative if one wants to do more than just store metals. If one wants to trade and invest, foreign banks offer even more choices than American banks or brokers. The best foreign banks are at home in any major currency, stock or bond exchange.

Starting from the beginning, though, if one is contemplating opening a foreign bank account, it is probably for one of five reasons. In his usual pithy way, Harry Browne sums up what these are (in his June 13, 1984 issue of <u>Harry Browne's Special Reports</u>, $225 per year to P.O. Box 5586, Austin, TX 78763).

"Most likely, your situation is roughly one of the following:

> "1. You have no interest in evading taxes or in hiding anything from the government or from anyone else. However, you've decided it would be useful to have a Swiss bank account--possibly because you think it's prudent to keep part of your

assets outside of the country in which you live. Or . . .

2. You don't want to break laws or evade taxes, but you would like to keep your affairs as private as possible. You're willing to report all your financial affairs to the government if required to do so, but not to anyone else. It may be that you want to shield your business from creditors, business associates, or relatives. Or . . .

3. You don't want to evade taxes because evasion could get you into a lot of trouble, and so you report all your income. But you also don't want the government or anyone else to know what the future will bring. I've found that most Swiss bank customer are in this category. Or . . .

4. You don't want to evade taxes but you DO evade them--simply because you can't report all your taxable income without disclosing other information you want to keep private. (There are ways of getting out of this category and safely into category #3, and they'll be discussed in this article.) Or . . .

5. You are a tax-evader by intention--and hope to hide a lot of money or to make a lot of money through your Swiss bank account, none of which ever will be reported to the government."

Obviously, each person must decide which of these scenarios best describes his or her particular situation. Whatever one does, one must be comfortable with it. As Browne puts it, "You can get into trouble for breaking the law. The risks are reasonable only for people who are desperate or unusually ambitious, who can handle risks emotionally, and who have first determined the exact terms of the law and the penalties involved."

Ultimately, the decision must be one's own. Browne continues, "No one can tell you whether or not you should break the law. That's a complicated matter that ultimately comes back to your own personal considerations of duty, risks, rewards, nerves, financial position, public exposure, and just plain feelings."

"Anyone who tells you that you MUST obey the law is ridiculous. I'm sure such a person would have had a lot to say in Nazi Germany.

"And anyone who tells you that you MUST break the law is just as ridiculous. Your future is at stake: It isn't a matter to be decided by some other person's imperatives or cute slogans.

"It's solely your decision because no one else will face the consequences of your decision."

CHOOSING A HAVEN

If one decides on the foreign account route, the next step is to choose an appropriate privacy haven (or havens); one that best suits the needs of the particular individual.

It is always helpful, both as a research tool and as an aid to one's readers, to develop a sound set of criteria which can easily be applied to determine the location of the best haven. It is important to stress that this is a fluid situation. As will be seen, the best haven for one need may not be the best for another. For each of the countries examined in this report nine question were asked. These are discussed below. A value (from 1 to 5) was then assigned, based upon the country's performance, vis-a-vis each of these criteria. The specific rankings are shown in the table on pp. 106, together with brief comments on the salient features of each nation. Following this, a more in-depth look at a few of the better (or just better known) havens will be taken.

How strict are the secrecy laws?

Surprisingly, few havens have unambiguous bank-secrecy laws whereby all participants know exactly what information will be given foreign authorities under any particular set of circumstances. Some countries only have a non-legal tradition of secrecy; other have "confidentiality" laws where the local government has access to records but is itself sworn to secrecy--a promise that may or may not be kept. Some have laws that are not always enforced; others have laws with loopholes. And not a few are tax havens without pretense to any secrecy laws.

How long a tradition has the haven had?

Length of tradition is vital. It is a safe bet that a country with several centuries' experience, like

Switzerland, or even several decades, like Luxembourg, won't be in as much of a hurry to change as havens such as Vanuatu in the Pacific, which only recently proclaimed itself. In all probability, the longer the tradition, the safer the haven.

Please note that the length of time a country has been a haven either in taxes or in banking secrecy is what is being considered here. The Channel Islands, for example, have a long tradition of the former but not of the latter.

Does its haven status have local support?

Put another way, do the haven's citizens also use the facilities? There's a world of difference in this regard between the Bahamas, where locals seem almost resentful of the haven provisions, and Austria, where average citizens regularly use the completely anonymous "password account," discussed in this report and, thus, have a vested interest in its continued existence.

Is the haven stable?

Any financial haven must also be a haven in non-financial ways. It must have a high degree of personal freedom. For example, income tax is abolished in North Korea and Albania and there is legal banking secrecy in Hungary (for Westerners, that is), but most individuals would rather go elsewhere, thank you. Of course, even free-market havens are not always stable. For example, Britain is, unfortunately, caving in to China's demands on Hong Kong, ostensibly abandoning its citizens to the 1997 deadline. Peking's promise to keep up the colony's tax haven status beyond that point seems dubious. Lebanon has very strict banking secrecy but is unstable. And there are degrees of stability: the Bahamas, Bermuda, Panama, and Costa Rica are less stable than Switzerland, Austria and Luxembourg.

Is it important to Washington?

Panama and Costa Rica, even though they are in an unstable area, enjoy the favor of the U.S. government. The U.S. wants to preserve Central American stability, at least, in the pro-Western nations there. Haven income is important to these countries and presumably Washington won't want to lean too hard on its strategic allies. And, since the CIA is known to have used Liechtenstein Anstalts for its flexibility and secrecy, it's inconceivable that the U.S. would want to wipe out that country's haven status. The Cayman Islands, on the other hand, has no strategic value to Washington. Indeed it is considered a royal pain in the backside.

Does it wave a "red flag"?

There are high-profile havens and low-profile havens. High-profile havens are scarcely known for anything else but promoting tax avoidance. Thus, any public dealing with them raises a "red flag" in tax collectors' offices around the world. The Caymans, Panama, and Liechtenstein are examples of "red flag" countries. Switzerland is in the second tier, while Austria and Luxembourg are another step below that level. Bermuda is lower still, but it can't offer the secrecy the others do.

A high profile doesn't necessarily mean trouble: Panama, being important enough, will be left alone. And otherwise high-profile nations, like Switzerland, that at least try to cooperate civilly with the U.S., even though they won't violate their own laws, are looked upon much more favorably than nations, such as the Cayman Islands, with which Washington enjoys less than cordial relations.

In any case, to remain consistent with the 1 to 5 rating, a number will be given to measure the "absence of a red flag." Zero is "reddest"; five means the country offers a very low profile.

Does it protect its sovereignty?

Has the haven caved in to the demands of the great powers, even in nonfinancial matters? The Dominican Republic has bank-secrecy laws, but when "turncoat" CIA agent Edwin Wilson travelled there incognito recently, he didn't expect U.S. agents to be tipped off and waiting for him, ready to immediately hustle him back to the U.S. There were no legal extradition formalities. U.S. agents operated in the Dominican Republic as they would Kansas City. Recently, with the Marcos and the Dennis Levine Insider Trading cases, Switzerland has shown that it is not as safe as was previously thought.

How efficient and convenient are the services?

Is there a large, competent staff available to serve the customer? The Cayman Islands may have high marks in some respects, but the staffs at many of its banks sometimes take a day to perform functions that Swiss bankers might do in an hour.

Also, how well does the bank staff speak the customer's language? Even though English is the world's investment language, for some bankers, English is not only a second language, but a distant second at that. By the same token, if one's native tongue is Spanish or French, many havens--especially in former British colonies--might be difficult to deal with. Again, Switzerland scores high in this respect, as most Swiss bankers speak at least four languages.

Finally, how convenient is the haven for one to deal with? It's best to visit one's money periodically, and so much the better if it's in a place that one enjoys visiting.

What taxes are levied on the haven's users?

This criterion was put in last because in some respects it is the least important. The first requirement of a haven is that it offer capital preservation. Nonetheless, to include a haven country which scores heavily in capital preservation but which also has high withholding, corporate, estate or other taxes, is to ignore an important consideration. Of course, there are several havens which essentially levy little or no taxes on non-residents. (See, for example, Austria)

COUNTRY RANKINGS

0 = Lowest, 5 = Highest, ? = Too soon to tell

Column 1 = Strictness of Secrecy Laws
Column 2 = Length of Tradition
Column 3 = Local Support
Column 4 = Stability
Column 5 = Importance to Washington
Column 6 = Absence of "Red Flag"
Column 7 = Protection of Sovereignty
Column 8 = Efficiency and Convenience
Column 9 = Tax Level
Column 10 = Total

Country	1	2	3	4	5	6	7	8	9	10
Austria	5	4	5	4	4	5	5	4	3	39
Bahamas	4	2	2	2	1	2	3	3	5	24
Bermuda	1	3	3	3	4	4	4	4	5	31
Cayman Islands	4	2	4	5	0	0	3	3	5	26
Channel Islands	0	4	4	5	1	4	4	5	3	30

Hong Kong	+ 5	+ 4	+ 5	+ 2	+ 3	+ 4	+ 4	+ 4	+ 4	+ 35
Isle of Man	+ 5	+ 2	+ 5	+ 5	+ 1	+ 5	+ 3	+ 5	+ 3	+ 34
Liechtenstein	+ 5	+ 4	+ 5	+ 5	+ 4	+ 0	+ 5	+ 4	+ 4	+ 36
Luxembourg	+ 5	+ 4	+ 4	+ 4	+ 4	+ 4	+ 3	+ 3	+ 2	+ 33
Panama	+ 5	+ 3	+ 4	+ 2	+ 5	+ 0	+ 5	+ 3	+ 4	+ 31
Singapore	+ 2	+ 3	+ 3	+ 3	+ 3	+ 5	+ 4	+ 4	+ 4	+ 31
Switzerland	+ 5	+ 5	+ 4	+ 5	+ 5	+ 1	+ 4	+ 5	+ 2	+ 36

Please Note: The subjectivity involved in any ranking system can always lead to arguable results, but two important point need to be made:

(1) All criteria have been given equal weight, even though their importance may well vary for different individuals. As a personal preference, the author feels that banking-secrecy laws are of paramount importance and that local tax levels are of relatively little importance. Some investors may feel the "red flag" criterion of little importance if, in choosing a haven, they plan to "hold all correspondence" and tell absolutely no one of their plans. Similarly, those who don't plan to visit the haven they use, who speak several languages or who plan to leave their investments sitting idle (with no need therefore, for efficient banking services) may rank efficiency and convenience as of negligible importance.

(2) One factor can drastically alter the entire suitability of a haven. Until recently, Grenada would have had a different sovereignty rating and was certainly of

little importance to Washington. Similarly, in the case of Hong Kong, if the Chinese do take over in 1997, this haven will, in all likelihood, disappear.

Now, these numerical grades are subjective. However, people like to see such grades, and they do give some idea of the relative standings.

HOW THEY RANK

Austria	39
Switzerland	36
Liechtenstein	36
Hong Kong	35
Isle of Man	34
Luxembourg	33
Bermuda	31
Singapore	31
Panama	31
Channel Islands	30
Cayman Islands	26
Bahamas	24

Following is a brief overview to the havens just ranked, plus comments on seventeen additional entities that are commonly promoted as "havens" but in reality are unsuitable for the needs of most people seeking offshore diversification. Then a closer look at Switzerland and several others will taken.

ANDORRA rates a perfect score on its internal tax level: it levies no taxes. However, it has no secrecy laws nor can it protect its sovereignty, because its rulers are the President of France and a Spanish Bishop, nor is it of any importance to Washington.

ANTIGUA is like many of the former British colonies in the Caribbean. It doesn't really protect its sovereignty and it has a reputation for sleazy conduct. However, it's highly rated in its importance to Washington, mostly because of the 1983 Grenada invasion. Antigua was one of the countries that sent troops to aid in the invasion.

AUSTRIA offers the lowest of profiles, being associated with many things other than its banking-secrecy laws. It ranks high on local support because many Austrians use the anonymous account. Overall, it is an impressive country, particularly from the red-flag aspect.

THE BAHAMAS may be a little more important to Washington than, say, the Cayman Islands--but not much more. Recently, the country has been less than perfect in protecting its sovereignty. And, this could get worse because of its overwhelming dependence on Washington. There are virtually no internal taxes.

BAHRAIN is a relatively new haven and has no secrecy laws.

BARBADOS has little haven tradition. However, it is very stable.

BERMUDA rates a perfect score on taxes, but has no bank-secrecy law.

THE BRITISH VIRGIN ISLANDS is currently involved in an imbroglio with U.S. tax authorities. It waves a big red flag, isn't important to Washington, and has no secrecy laws. If the U.S. Congress follows through on its threat to make the U.S. Virgin Islands a better tax haven, such an action would probably remove the only advantage that the British Virgin Islands has over its neighbor at present.

THE CAYMAN ISLANDS is important to Washington--but only in the most negative sense. The strictness of its secrecy laws makes it a focal point for much of the anti-haven feeling in Washington. Yet, these secrecy laws are in doubt now that the July 1986 treaty has been signed with the U.S. Therefore, while the Cayman Islands is a stable country internally and has good local support, its high profile and lack of importance to Washington indicate that it may be a possible source of problems in the future.

THE CHANNEL ISLANDS, like Bermuda, makes no pretense of being a bank secrecy haven. It is a tax haven and it's very efficient. The country is of little value to Washington, but the important thing is that it has no secrecy law. In fact, it will cooperate with any government that comes to it with the tax problems of one of its nationals.

COSTA RICA might strengthen its bank-secrecy laws if there were not such strong laws in neighboring Panama. It's important to Washington and isn't really a "red flag" country. However, in terms of banking, it can't hold a candle to Panama.

CYPRUS is the Singapore of the Middle East, trying to take Lebanon's place. However, since the Turkish Cypriots broke away and declared an independent state in November of 1983, Cyprus itself is now faced with instability. Most importantly, it has no long tradition, no secrecy laws, and is only a tax haven in certain areas.

THE DOMINICAN REPUBLIC doesn't even try to protect its sovereignty, at least in matters concerning the U.S. It's very close to the U.S. and has permitted that country to treat its territory as it would any American city. The CIA Edwin Wilson case is a good example of this.

EL SALVADOR speaks for itself. It's very important to Washington but is not at all stable or efficient. To bank on the future of a country like this is to ask for trouble.

GRENADA never had bank-secrecy laws, and even though it recently became important to Washington, one certainly wouldn't call it stable. Nor can it effectively protect its sovereignty.

HONG KONG rates very highly in every category except in stability and its importance to Washington. Were it not for the end of British sovereignty, it could be the most stable country in the world. However, Hong Kong's future after June 30, 1997 is very, very clouded. All the best people are making plans to emigrate. While the country is not really important to Washington as such, it rates a three because it is a conduit to Communist China in much the same way as Switzerland is to Communist Europe. Hong Kong is also an economic giant. But, in short, it's a great haven with a cloudy future.

THE ISLE OF MAN shows great promise, scoring well in almost every respect. Keep this one in mind.

JORDAN is much like Cyprus, although perhaps more stable. However, it is in a very volatile area.

LEBANON did have a lot going for it but can no longer protect its sovereignty nor, more importantly, its stability.

LIBERIA is in some ways a tax haven but it has no secrecy laws at all. The country also lacks stability.

LUXEMBOURG rates very high. Its main drawbacks are that it's a member of the Common Market, and that it may not be able to protect its sovereignty. Luxembourg is basically a socialist country so tax levels are high and it's not as efficient as it could be. On the other hand, it is a fairly low profile country, few people know about it.

MONTSERRAT is a high-profile tax haven which seems to attract dubious business. Like most Caribbean havens, it rates low on banking secrecy laws.

THE NETHERLAND ANTILLES is not really impressive in any category except that of the internal tax levels. It's more efficient to deal with than many other Caribbean islands, but offers neither bank-secrecy laws nor much stability.

PANAMA'S saving grace is that, despite its high profile, it is very important to Washington. This fact aside, it's not particularly efficient. Also, the country raises the reddest flag of all to the I.R.S.

SINGAPORE doesn't rate badly in any category. Time will tell if it will succeed in its quest to become another Hong Kong. At the moment it has no red flag, probably because it has no real secrecy laws.

ST. VINCENT is the prototypical Caribbean island. It's above average on its internal taxes but it's not that stable, has no bank secrecy law, and little tradition.

SWITZERLAND is still the granddaddy of havens. But, as the next section will make clear, it's not what it used to be. For most of the readers of this book, however, it is still very valuable.

TURKS AND CAICOS is the new boy on the block. The rating on local support is of questionable value simply because there are so few inhabitants that this criterion is difficult to measure. Similarly, because it's such a backwater, its sovereignty has not really been put to the test, although being a British Colony it could arguably rate a two or three in this category. Turks and Caicos' isolation paradoxically gives it a high profile. It offers virtually nothing except its budding tax and bank-secrecy laws. Thus, any company seen registering in this backwater must, in all likelihood, be there to evade or avoid taxes.

VANUATU raises the reddest of red flags. It has a good internal tax level. However, it is very hard to get to, being dependent on Australia at present for an air link and has no strategic importance to either Australia or the U.S.

The Decline of Switzerland

The biggest change of the past few years--since about 1983--is that (according to these criteria) Switzerland is no longer the absolute best place to deal through internationally. As of 1986, the number one spot belongs to Austria, a less well-publicized haven, which, in fact, had been number two after Switzerland prior to this.

Why has Switzerland declined in the past several years? In three vital areas, the country has changed to the detriment of its perfect haven status.

Perhaps the most disturbing area is in Switzerland's failure to protect its sovereignty. Insider trading is an effective case in point. Switzerland essentially allowed itself to be forced by the U.S. government into changing its law to make insider trading a crime, something it had never been. It is important to remember that, when a criminal offense--under Swiss law--has taken place, Swiss banking secrecy does not hold. So, by changing its law to conform with U.S. statutes, Switzerland shot itself in the proverbial foot. It got nothing in exchange from the U.S. Moreover, in making insider trading a crime, the Swiss departed from the European tradition that views this activity as a fact of business life. In countries where insider trading is legal, e.g., the U.K. and Austria, the authorities take the position that, since some people are insiders in business, they will always know certain things before outsiders do. Furthermore, these insiders ought to be able to act on their knowledge to insure efficient markets.

This attitude seems to be the most sane, realistic way of approaching insider trading. Drawn to its logical conclusion, making insider trading a crime will paralyze market makers. They will be afraid to act on any information that the market reveals to them.

And indeed, this absurd situation occurred after the big Levine affair in the summer of 1986. A hot-shot Wall street mergers and acquisitions specialist, Dennis B. Levine (a former managing director of Drexel Burnham Lambert), was discovered to have made millions by acting on inside information in buying the stocks and options of certain companies. Levine pleaded guilty to four felony charges in June 1986 in the largest insider trading case in history. After the S.E.C. threw the book at him, a pall settled over his colleagues. Five of his closest associates also went to jail. Many on Wall Street know that they themselves have done the same thing that Levine was convicted of, though not to the same degree. When the situation arises that deal makers are afraid to talk to anyone, it can only damage the smooth functioning of the U.S. economy.

But enough moralizing. For the purpose of this text, it is instructive to see how Levine operated and how he was caught. Levine used the Bahamas branch of Switzerland's oldest bank, Bank Leu. He made only day trips to Nassau, and almost certainly with the knowledge and help of bank officers, he collaborated with them to break U.S. insider trading laws. When U.S. officials began to suspect the Nassau branch of the Bank Leu office they demanded to know whether Levine had an account there.

Remember, according to Swiss law, it is a crime for a bank to reveal this information unless there is positive evidence showing that the alleged client committed criminal acts. In this case, the crime was insider trading. However, U.S. authorities had no proof that Levine was trading on inside information. They needed the Bank Leu records to prove their accusations. All the authorities had was a strong suspicion that Levine was using Bank Leu's Bahamian branch.

So, in such a case, no Swiss bank should have been obligated to hand over client records. In fact, under

Swiss law, the bank in question is prohibited from turning over client records unless, again, strong evidence of criminal activity is brought forth.

And yet Bank Leu gave the U.S. authorities all the information they wanted. In essence it gave them their case against Levine, rather than the other way around. Why? Basically because Washington used a carrot and stick approach. If Bank Leu would spill the beans, said the S.E.C., it would be granted immunity from prosecution. If it wouldn't turn over the necessary documents, well, there is, after all, that New York branch office of the Bank Leu . . . . The threat of having its U.S. assets frozen was enough to make Leu talk.

Bank Leu's decision was greeted with dismay by old-style Swiss bankers. They saw it as yet another sign that Swiss banking secrecy is not what it used to be. Many of them point to the fact that, since Switzerland has become a bigger international capital center than ever before, this has meant more ties to, or dependence on, the other big centers, New York being, of course, the largest.

In the past, Swiss banking was almost entirely an insular industry, concerned simply with preserving and managing its clients' money. The typical client was usually a wealthy individual, not an institution. Swiss banks, of course, still do this, but, more and more, the large ones are becoming major players in the international capital markets, underwriting stock offerings, for instance.

Since these newer activities depend on close ties with New York, the participating Swiss banks have much to lose if they are frozen out of the U.S. markets. They've become much more willing to sacrifice individual clients to protect themselves.

It should be noted here that this new breed of Swiss banker is disheartening, even disgusting, to the old school, which believes that a bank's first, last, and only responsibility is to its client. Unfortunately, this is a view that is becoming increasingly antiquated among Swiss bankers.

The Levine case is just the latest in a series of incidents that have affected Switzerland's reputation. The case of former Philippine dictator Ferdinand Marcos is well known. When Marcos fled the Philippines, he left pertinent papers behind documenting the existence, but not the size, of several Swiss bank accounts. Following normal procedure, to repeat, the new government would not only have to show that Marcos was engaged in criminal activities but that these activities were also crimes in Switzerland. This would not have been too difficult to do, as a good case for fraud and embezzlement could be made. However, rather than following normal legal procedure which prescribes waiting for the evidence to be presented, the

Swiss Federal Council (the highest governing body in the country) voted to freeze all Marcos' assets even before the new Manila government presented its case. This was done because Marcos apparently attempted to withdraw or transfer certain funds. It was the first time in Swiss history that accounts were frozen in this way. In the Duvalier case a few weeks later, the Swiss, stung by the adverse reaction of domestic bankers to the Marcos affair, waited until evidence was formally presented before freezing the ex-Haitian dictator's accounts.

One can plausibly put forth the argument that the Swiss were morally bound to freeze the assets that these dictators had obviously looted, both from their own people and the American taxpayer. Were the U.S. in the same situation, it would most certainly have done the same thing.

But it bears remarking that this approach represents the latest stage in the slow evolution of Swiss banking attitudes. After World War II, ex-Nazis were able to keep their money safe in Switzerland, despite intense outside pressures. After the death of Ethiopian Emperor Selassi and the fall of the Shah of Iran, the new governments of both countries tried to get their hands on that part of their former leaders' wealth alleged to be in Switzerland. The Swiss, however, never even admitted (if that is the right word) that the two men had Swiss bank accounts. This took place in the late 1970's. The past few years have marked a distinct change from this policy.

Returning to the evaluation criteria, it is clear that Switzerland is not protecting its sovereignty as well now as it did a few years back. While it would have rated a perfect "5" then, it only qualifies for a "3" now. In two other areas the Swiss also seem to be slipping, although the detection of this slippage cannot be measured as objectively in these areas as in the first. Until a few years ago, Switzerland rated a perfect score in the important category of "Local Support." The best havens being places where the local citizenry supports the country's privacy provisions and, ideally, makes use of the banking operation these provisions protect.

Local support is still very strong in Switzerland. In 1984, in fact, a Socialist sponsored referendum to dilute banking secrecy lost by a 3 to 1 margin. But what often happens in Switzerland is that--to keep social peace--the winners in any vote will subtly co-opt some of the losers' ideas to effect a compromise. It seems that this also happened in the area of bank secrecy. Since a substantial minority of the Swiss people don't want bank secrecy laws to protect dictators like Marcos, the government responded quickly when the affair came up. Thus while the average Swiss citizens still believe in the idea of banking secrecy, he wants limits to it. Therefore, Switzerland receives a "4", one less than perfect, in this category. Finally, Switzerland has always been a "red flag" country, as far as the tax authorities are concerned. It has long been known as a bank secrecy haven. In the past few years, however, the flag presented to tax authorities has gotten even redder.

All the forgoing should not be construed as a warning to avoid Switzerland. In many respects, and for most people, Swiss banks, or at least those with assets beyond the reach of the U.S. government, still offer excellent service and a high level of secrecy. While dictators and insider traders can no longer expect protection under Swiss law, the policy in other areas has not changed. For instance, tax evasion remains a civil offense, not a criminal one. There have been no cases of Swiss banks breaking down walls of secrecy to comply with governments' requests for information on tax evaders. The Swiss realize that compliance with such demands would irretrievably damage their status as a haven. As a result, they are unwilling to provide any help.

In the next section, Austria, the country that has now replaced Switzerland as the world's best haven, will be examined in depth. Nevertheless, there are still many things that Switzerland can do better than Austria, or, indeed any one else in the world.

Because of its virtually impregnable defense system, Switzerland remains the best place to physically store precious metals. Gold has never been illegal in Switzerland, and almost certainly never will be confiscated. Austrian banks storing metals do so in the duty-free zones of Zurich.

In addition, if one is a wealthy investor (upwards of $1 million) Switzerland's private banks offer an efficiency of service that is unmatched anywhere else in the world. Even for smaller investors, the quality of service is probably better than that for comparably-sized accounts in other countries. Furthermore, for those desiring some sort of funds management, the internationally-minded Swiss bankers are probably in the best position to roam the world's markets looking for superior investment opportunities. Portfolio management is rare in the other top havens.

Finally, one can take advantage of Swiss efficiency, turning the potential disadvantage of close ties to world financial markets into a variety of subtle methods for repatriating funds. As will be seen in a later chapter, it is possible to use a credit card, tied to a Swiss bank account, to privately transfer funds anywhere in the world. Indeed, this is just one minor, but rarely mentioned, advantage offered by the Swiss. For centuries, they have performed this aspect of banking--money transfer--far more efficiently than any one else. Certainly this was recognized by the mid-18th century. When King Louis XVI of France was involved in the financial crisis that eventually precipitated the French Revolution, he turned to the Geneva banker, Jacques Necker (the father of Madame de Stael), to try to sort things out. During the 19th century, Zurich gradually superceded Geneva as Switzerland's main financial center, a position it still holds today.

Most Swiss banks are "full-service" banks; that is, not only is it possible to open the familiar checking or savings account, but these banks can also perform a variety of other financial services for the individual (e.g., buying and selling precious metals, securities, CDs, futures and options).

The author's top recommendation among Swiss banks is the Foreign Commerce Bank. This bank tailors its services to smaller-scale, English-speaking clients with a predominant interest in precious metals. (One note of interest, the Foreign Commerce Bank stores metals in its client's name, unlike most other Swiss banks.)

These are just a few of the many examples of the valuable services that Swiss banks provide. Switzerland still is, in fact, the preferred haven for most of the world's frightened individuals. If this report seems less enthusiastic about Switzerland than in the past, it reflects the author's dismay in seeing a haven, long accustomed to unquestioned premier status, lose some of its allure. Of course, who is to say that the events of recent months will not prove to be an aberration? Perhaps Switzerland will begin to better protect its sovereignty and return to the old ways of banking. But even if it doesn't, there is no reason for anyone, aside of insider traders, drug dealers, and dictators, to consider pulling out of Switzerland. Perhaps Swiss banks can now be best used in conjunction with Austrian ones which, in turn, have their own particular advantages.

Foreign Commerce Bank: Precious Metals Accounts

Silver Bullion

Minimum initial investment: U.S. $5,000 or equivalent. No minimum for additional purchases. Available in ounces. 1% commission on purchases and sales. Storage and insurance provided in Zurich at 0.4% per year, charged quarterly on value of average holdings.

Silver Coins

U.S. silver coins of 1964 or earlier are available in bags of U.S. $1,000 face value, containing Dimes and/or Quarters. Pure silver content per bag: 720 troy ounces. Minimum initial investment: one bag. Storage and insurance is provided through brokers in New York at U.S. $30 per bag per year.

Gold Coins

All current coins available. For U.S. Double Eagles, British Sovereigns, Mexican 50 Pesos, Austrian 110 Coronas, and Krugerrands, the bank offers special accounts. Minimum initial investment: U.S. $5,000 or equivalent. No minimum for additional purchases. Storage and insurance: 0.3% per year, charged quarterly on value of average holdings.

Gold Bullion

Minimum initial investment: U.S. $5,000 or equivalent. No minimum for additional purchases. Available in ounces. 1/2 % commission on purchases and sales. Storage and insurance: 0.3 per year, charged quarterly on value of average holdings.

Platinum

Minimum initial investment: U.S. $5,000 or equivalent. No minimum for additional purchases and sales. Storage and insurance: 0.3% per year, charged quarterly on value of average holdings.

Palladium

Minimum initial investment: U.S. $5,000 or equivalent. No minimum for additional purchases. Available in ounces. 1/2% commission on purchases and sales. Storage and insurance: 0.3% per year, charged quarterly on value of average holdings.

Other Precious Metals

Upon request.

Financing

All precious metals may be purchased on margin. The maximum financing available is 50% of their market value.

Account Facilities

All accounts may be opened in the name of one or more individuals. They can be established in U.S. $, SFr., DM, & HFL, and Can.$

These conditions are subject to change without prior notice. *February 1, 1983.

Austria

All of a sudden, Austria has become, perhaps, the most interesting place in which to bank internationally. Measured by the nine criteria, it is currently the best haven in the world. Austria now has even stronger banking secrecy laws and practices than neighboring secrecy haven, Switzerland. Austrian banks probably have the greatest local support--and local use--of any haven. The country has not caved in to demands that it change its laws on insider trading or its policies regarding the freezing of dictators' accounts. This is probably because the country has such a low profile that neither flamboyant insider traders nor any dictators have yet used it, or, at least, if they have, no foreign power has yet tried to prosecute them there.

Nevertheless, even those individuals who are neither corrupt dictators nor insider traders have reason to be interested in Austria. It has just abolished its last remaining withholding tax on Austrian schilling interest, and has long been free of any tax on Swiss franc deposits. (Switzerland levies a 35% withholding tax on interest.) Austria is a very stable, low profile country which nonetheless has started to gear its services to foreign investors. It is very probable that, in the next five to ten years, the advantages of Austria will become much more well known. For now, though, only a lucky few are aware of them.

Politically, Austria is changing in refreshing ways. Outside the country the recent presidential vote was seen in terms of Kurt Waldheim's Nazi past. But Austrians, both Waldheim supporters and his Socialist opponents, saw the vote as an unprecedented and stunning defeat for an incumbent socialist presidency of nearly two decades. Immediately after the election the Socialist head of government resigned (President Waldheim is only a ceremonial head of state). His replacement, Franz Vrantizkly, is on the far right wing of the Socialist party. Vrantizkly wants to cut state spending drastically and speaks admiringly of both the Graham Rudman Hollings bill and tax cuts, in general.

It's clear that the Socialists are making a last-ditch effort to stay in power after the parliamentary elections next spring. In fact, they're now trying to be more conservative than their conservative opponents. In spite of this, the Socialists will probably lose out in next year's elections. But, no matter who wins, the much welcomed result should be the reform of Austria's bloated welfare state.

The Austrian Socialists whom the author knows personally--citizens who have kept the Socialist government in power for years--are somewhat extraordinary in their attitudes. For instance, one couple (the wife is a doctor--G.P.--and the husband is a physics teacher) always voted Socialists but were completely up in arms a few years ago about a government withholding tax on interest from the super-secret "password" accounts. These are bank accounts which require only a number and an agreed-upon password to make a deposit or withdrawal. (In Switzerland, the banks have to know every client's identity.) It's an open secret that these accounts--in existence for decades--are methods by which Austrians (and foreigners banking in Austria)--safely store "black" or undeclared money. It is also a fact that "nearly every Austrian" according to the above mentioned couple--themselves included--has these accounts.

The government's proposal to withhold a part of the interest payments in tax was shouted down by "nearly every Austrian" and eventually dropped. In fact, all kinds of bank accounts are now free of withholding tax on interest.

One of the most important criteria in choosing a privacy haven is that there be broad local support for the secrecy provisions. Such support ensures that these provisions will remain strong and in place. According to this criterion, Austria has a distinct advantage over Switzerland. In that better-known secrecy haven, the Socialist party has for years been trying to abolish secrecy and, though defeated at the polls, has succeeded in watering it down.

In Austria, banking secrecy had been a tradition for at least two centuries before it was finally codified into law in 1979. Austrian banking secrecy is put forth in Section 23 of the Banking Act of February 20, 1979 ("Kreditwesengesetz"). This section states that "financial institutions, their shareholders, members of their boards, and their employees are not allowed to disclose or make use of any secrets entrusted or made available to them exclusively in the course of business relations with customers. If any facts which are subject to banking secrecy become known to officials or public authorities in the course of their official duties, such officials shall be bound by the official secrecy regulations and may be released from these only in the cases specified in paragraph 2. The obligation to observe banking secrecy is not subject to any time limit."

The text goes on to state that banking secrecy may be broken only in connection with criminal proceedings before the criminal court, probate proceedings before the probate court, or in the case of penal proceedings instituted because of deliberate offenses against tax law--excluding financial irregularities, i.e., tax evasion, which is not a criminal offense. There is a maximum jail term of one year in prison for transgressors compared to six months in Switzerland. But there are areas in which Austrian laws could be improved to be more like Swiss laws.

First, disclosure of secrets by negligence is not illegal in Austria, while it is in Switzerland. It must be proven that an employee acted with specific intent either to harm or to benefit. As one can imagine, there are many sets of circumstances in which an employee could claim to have accidentally misplaced information and to prove otherwise would be difficult.

Another foible of Austrian law is that prosecution of alleged breaches of secrecy can only take place after the bank's client makes a complaint. After both the deed and its perpetrator are known, the victim has only a six-week period to submit a complaint to the criminal courts.

Finally, prosecution of bank-secrecy lapses is not carried out by the government, as in Switzerland, but rather by the individual victim.

On the plus side, secrecy is breached only very rarely (twice in a recent decade) and, then, only in cases involving Austrians--no non-residents have been involved as of yet. Nor have there been any cases of American authorities asking that the veil of secrecy be removed. Indeed, since insider trading is not a crime in Austria, unlike in Switzerland, the SEC would have gotten nowhere with bank authorities had Levine been using Austria. It is likely that Austria has been left alone because of its extraordinarily low profile when compared with such countries as the Caymans, Panama, the Bahamas and Switzerland--all nations with which the IRS has battled.

Furthermore, while Austria is one of those countries that taxes its citizens at a very high rate (hence making black "password" accounts popular with Austrians), it can be a no-tax haven for non-residents bringing money into the country. (Non-residents are those not living in Austria for more than three consecutive months. Yet even this requirement is interpreted loosely. Thus, nothing stops one from spending a day across the border every three months and still qualifying).

Non-residents are exempt from Austrian income, wealth, gift or inheritance taxes on monies deposited in Austria.

In addition, while there is a 20% sales tax on physical possession of gold and silver, this is refunded when tourists or non-residents leave the country with the material. Non-residents can also acquire any security with complete anonymity--even the bank doesn't know the purchaser's identity. All that is required is that one produce a valid passport, indicating non-resident status. No names or other information is taken.

Austria is more than just a tax and bank secrecy haven. Right now it happens to be a hot place to invest money. The Vienna Stock Exchange topped the world's markets in performance in 1985, rising in dollar terms by 187%. Furthermore, for those investors looking for a solid currency and high returns in a politically stable area, Austria and its schilling bonds have been hard to beat in the last year or so. The following discussion points up another advantage held by Austria: low minimums. Often these minimums are so low that any investor can take advantage of them. During the past 16 months, holders of Austrian government bonds have benefitted from the highest interest rate payments of any hard-currency country, as well as from having their asset denominated in that same hard currency. The Austrian schilling has been among the strongest currencies in the past five calendar quarters. In terms of exchange rate appreciation, the schilling has held its own against such heavy hitters as the German mark and Swiss franc. Yet the total return from schilling bonds has been higher than the bonds of these other two countries.

With foreign currency bonds, one can enjoy a "triple-play" during the best of times, now, for instance. First, as with regular bonds, one gains with the interest rate, which is a fixed amount paid to the bond holder regardless of what happens to the market interest rate after the bond's purchase. During times of high interest rates, one can "lock-in" high yields. Second, if market interest rates drop after one buys the bond, its price rises. In Austria, rates have been falling since early 1985. Finally, if the currency in which the bonds are denominated rises against one's own currency, profits increase accordingly.

The following gives an indication of how the bonds of each of three major "hard currency" governments--Austria, Switzerland and Germany--have done, in U.S.-Dollar terms, since the end of February-early March 1985, when the U.S. dollar was at its peak.

The three bonds chosen are the German mark 7-1/4% World Bank 1983-1993 (February 27, 1985: 96-3/4, June 2, 1985: 104-3/4)

Price rise 8.3%

Price plus yield

for period held 9.1%

Swiss franc 5-1/4% Republic of Austria 1977-1991 (March 6, 1985: 99-1/2, May 29, 1986: 101-1/2

Price rise 2.0%

Price plus yield

for period held: 8.6%

Austrian schilling 10-1/2 Investitions-Anleihe 1982-1992 (February 26, 1985: 109, May 28, 1986: 110-1/4

Price rise: 1.1%

Price rise plus

yield for period held: 13.4%

As one can see, while the schilling bond lagged behind the other two in terms of aggregate price rise, when its higher coupon yield is added in, it is the top performer.

Currently, Austrian bonds retain their interest rate edge. Their coupon is 7%, compared with 6% for German Mark Eurobonds and 5% for Swiss Franc Eurobonds.

Add to this the recent exchange rate histories of these three currencies, and one sees how very well schilling bonds have done.

From February 26, 1985 to May 15, 1986 the Austrian schilling soared 58.5% from its initial level of 4.1 U.S. cents. Since the schilling is tied to the mark, it is not surprising that the mark rose 5.6 in this period, but bond returns still fell short due to the smaller coupon rate an Austrian schilling bond's total return would have been the best of the three. The total return on each of the three bonds--combining the three components is: Austrian schilling 71.9%, Swiss franc 68.7%, and German mark 67.7%.

Another overlooked advantage of Austrian schilling bonds is the low minimum investment needed to purchase them. Austrian banks require a Sfr. 10,000 (U.S. $5,300) or DM 10,000 (U.S. $4,500) minimum purchase. But for Austrian schilling bonds the minimum is AS 10,000 (actually ten bonds with a face value of AS 1,000 each). At current exchange rates this is only U.S. $611. Furthermore, it is often possible to finance one's purchases with a 75% margin loan.

So, theoretically, it is possible for clients to participate in the Austrian government bond market for roughly $150. This is extraordinarily accessible by any standards.

This play on bonds is but one example of the many opportunities offered by Austrian banks. Actually, one could even have brought Swiss franc bonds in Austria and been exempt from the 35% interest withholding tax which Switzerland levies. There is no interest tax on any Swiss franc deposits in Austria. It would have been impossible to get these returns on Swiss franc bonds had one used Swiss banks as intermediaries. They would have deducted

35% of the interest as tax. In theory, one can buy Austria schilling bonds through Switzerland, but in practice, Swiss bankers know very little about shilling investments. Austrian banks also offer checking and savings accounts in all other major currencies. Focobank (Austria) even offers checking accounts denominated in silver and gold, and tied directly to their prices. There are, in short, a whole range of possibilities. The author recently visited the headquarters of five Austrian banks. In all but one, where he was known, the author went in without an appointment saying that he was a potential new foreign depositor with about $100,000 to invest. The idea was to see how prepared each bank was to service the customer or at least to provide any required information.

Four of these banks are among the biggest in Austria. All publish literature luring foreign business. The fifth, Focobank (Austria), is a wholly-owned subsidiary of Foreign Commerce Bank of Zurich. It functions almost like a private bank, unlike either its larger Swiss owner or the other Austrian banks. Focobank is altogether different from the big banks, institutions where one cannot expect to get much personal service. Nevertheless, the best of these big banks may appeal to some investors, so the author's experiment might be of some interest to them. Two of these four banks can be dismissed immediately. Both have English-language literature, but neither seems prepared as of yet to properly service non-resident clients. These are the Landerbank (Am Hof 2,1010 Vienna) and the Genossenschaftliche Zentralbank (Herrengasse I, 1010 Vienna). The first is a naturalized bank run by Socialist party affiliates. Hence it is, in Austrian parlance, a "Red" bank, as opposed to the second, a "Black" or conservative bank, owned, in this case, by a farmer's cooperative. Landerbank has a brochure listing terms and conditions, but there is no information on precious metal. In addition, the bank representative with whom the author spoke appeared to be half asleep, obviously not concerned about recruiting new clients. And this is, in the third largest bank in Austria. Even this languor has a certain charm as it points out how low a profile Austrian banks keep. G. Zentralbank's people were all friendly and helpful, but the author was sent to four different departments in two different buildings before speaking to someone who knew anything about foreign account terms and conditions. And even this person had to read the information from a handwritten paper, as there was no printed literature. One bank representative also said, "We discourage physical gold. If someone wants to buy gold shares we'll do it."

The two other banks visited were far more interesting. Again, one is "Black" and one is "Red." The non-nationalized bank, the second largest in Austria, is

Girozentrale (Schubertring 5, 1011 Vienna, telephone (222) 72-94). It is owned by member savings banks. It features, on premise, gold coin storage. All coins are stored in envelopes, which are stamped with the owner's name and are the owner's legal property. There is a two-coin minimum, but only the Mapleleaf was available the day that the author visited, as the Krugerrand had been discontinued. (Only legal-tender coins like these are tax-free when stored in Austria.) The annual storage charge is DM 1.50 (about 60 cents) per coin for the accounts opened in one's own name and DM 3 per year per coin for the anonymous numbered gold coin accounts. (There is a 20 Mapleleaf minimum with these accounts.) The bank has a full service branch in London where numbered or password accounts can also be opened and maintained. As with all Austrian banks, non-residents stopping in at the London branch (Morgan House I, Angle Court) need only present their passports to prove that they are non-residents. No names are taken by the banks. The ability to get Austrian banking services in London may appeal to people, as the U.K. is more accessible than Austria. There are three potential drawbacks to this bank, however. First of all, as with other large banks, one won't get personal service. Second, the bank does not offer silver and gold bullion accounts. Finally, unlike all other banks mentioned here, Girozentrale has a minimum account size AS 250,000 ($17,000), which is not negligible.

Almost certainly the most useful of the big banks is the biggest bank in Austria, Creditanstalt (head office Schottengasse 6, 1010 Vienna, (222) 66-220). At this bank, the minimum is a mere AS 300 ($18). Because Creditanstalt is a big bank, the author had to go to different offices to get information about different areas (e.g., new accounts, securities, precious metals). Once at the correct locale everyone was efficient and friendly, but asking directions at the central table was like questioning a government bureaucrat. Creditanstalt is 60% state-owned, but much more efficient and well-run than fellow "Red" Landerbank. Although, according to Creditanstalt's precious metals department, few of its clients are interested in gold, the bank does have good facilities for on-site storage: closed envelopes in the clients name, with no minimums at a nominal storage cost of AS 50 ($3) per year per envelope as well as a handling charge of AS 100 each time one wants to deposit or withdraw coins.

As under the current, but rather absurd, Austrian laws, banks cannot store bullion in Austria without charging tax, Creditanstalt offers gold and silver accounts at its Zurich affiliate bank, Wirtschafts-und Privatbank. Unfortunately these accounts were not designed in a way that would appeal to a North American clientele. They are non-physical accounts where actual bullion is not set aside in the clients's name, but rather is stored in the bank's name. In any case, minimums are 30 ounces of gold or 300 ounces of silver respectively; storage charges are 2% and 2.2% for gold name and numbered accounts respectively; 3% and 3.2% for silver accounts. The bank has two foreign branches, which is both good news and bad news. The London branch (29 Grehsam) can do all the things Girozentrale's London branch can, although this is not spelled out in its brochures. But the second branch, because of its location in New York (717 Fifth Avenue), is somewhat handicapped. Generally, it is a good idea to stay away from foreign banks with a U.S. exposure because these banks could possibly be held hostage for their clients' secrets, as was Bank Leu. Of course this has never happened to the relatively low-profile CA nor to any other Austrian bank, but there is a first time for everything.

The Focobank is the last bank in the author's survey. Focobank (Austria) (Rathausstrase 20, P.O. Box 306, 1010 Vienna, (222) 43-61-61) is owned by the Foreign Commerce Bank of Zurich. While Foco (Austria) is owned by Foco Switzerland, it operates independently. The biggest difference between the two is that the Vienna bank essentially works with its clients as a private banker. Each client is assigned either one or two bankers to handle all requests. At the other banks in the survey, a functional departmental structure is used (i.e., a securities order would go to that department, etc.).

Focobank is perhaps the most liquid bank in Austria, and the only one to provide the Swiss-style liquidity information used by Harry Browne in his bank ratings. At year-end 1985, this figure was a flush 125%, according to bank statements.

Focobank (Austria) offers the best range of metal accounts of any Austrian bank. For silver, gold, platinum and palladium, the minimum opening purchase is U.S. $3,000. Commissions are 1% per trade on silver, 1/2% on the rest. There are no minimums nor commissions for coins. More important is the storage method. For coins held on the premises, the big banks are actually cheaper. Foco's annual fees are 0.35% of the coins' market value. But no other Austrian bank stores physical bullion in the client's name. This is done in the Zurich Duty-Free Zone. Storage on silver is 0.35%, for all other metals it's 0.25%. Focobank specializes in low premium Austrian 100 Koronas. Metals on margin and forward contracts are also available.

Needless to say, all regular accounts and investments (i.e., password accounts, securities, currencies) are offered by the bank. There is no minimum account opening amount.

Focobank (Austria) and Creditanstalt are at present the only two Austrian banks that have decided to make things easy for international investors. As this haven becomes better known, though, more banks will probably jump into the fray.

For a low profile, low taxes, and high flexibility, Austria represents a significant opportunity.

The following are brief thumbnail sketches of some of the other havens:

<u>Liechtenstein</u>

This tiny principality of 61 square miles and 26,000 people governs itself but shares its currency, communications, and banking laws with Switzerland. It is almost certainly the most conservative nation in Europe (its citizens are widely known as "the rednecks of Europe"). Though this accounts for the fact that women still can't vote, it probably also accounts for the fact that there is as much financial freedom here as anywhere else in the world.

Liechtenstein offers moderate taxation, up to 20%. However, what makes Liechtenstein attractive is the ANSTALT, or Establishment, which is the perfect tax haven.

Anstalts are similar to holding companies. They can be founded for as little as Sfr. 30,000 (U.S. $13,800). All Anstalts pay 2% of contributed capital as a one-time incorporation tax. But ANSTALTS with no local activities pay no profits tax, and only a small annual net worth tax of one-tenth of 1.0% (0.1%), with a minimum Sfr. 1,000 charge.

Once established with the one required Liechtenstein board member (usually a caretaker lawyer), ANSTALTS can do virtually anything one can imagine a corporation doing--in total secrecy.

For world governments, this fact is a boon for their spy organizations, such as the KGB, MI5 or CIA, but a bane for their tax authorities' attempts to curb individuals' tax avoidance.

WAVING A RED FLAG. Therein lies a principal drawback of using ANSTALTS. They are the reddest of red flags to tax men. Any entity using one must include the word ANSTALT (German), Establishment (in English), or Etablissement (in French). So any international company with the name "Establishment" after it will have a very high profile indeed.

Not everyone needs an ANSTALT, and, for many, owning one is not worth the attendant headaches. ANSTALTS are usually used in conjunction with a Swiss bank, which can establish one for its customers if both decide that it would be worthwhile.

LIECHTENSTEIN'S BANK AND SAVINGS BANK LAW OF DECEMBER 21, 1960 (ARTICLE 47)

(1) Whoever intentionally

(a) ...

(b) as an organ, officer, bank employee, auditor or auditor's aide, member of the banking commission, or officer or employee of its secretariat shall infringe the duty of secrecy or divulge a professional secret, or whoever induces one to do so, or attempts to induce another to do so, shall be punished for the offense by a fine of up to twenty thousand francs or by imprisonment up to six months, or both.

(2) When acting negligently, the perpetrator shall be punished for the offense by a fine up to ten thousand francs.

Up until 1983, local governments had absolutely no knowledge of anything connected with ANSTALTS, not even their numbers. This situation changed slightly at year-end 1983. The new requirements forced all companies with a business purpose to present fully audited balance sheets to the authorities by June 30, 1984. However, companies with no commercial purpose except managing assets--and this includes most tax-avoidance ANSTALTS--did not have to comply. Although they did have to at least identify themselves, if only to say that they were concerned solely with money management. So the authorities now know at least how many of what type of companies operate out of Liechtenstein. And the new regulations will certainly keep local accountants busy.

After the 1977 Credit Suisse scandal, in which an ANSTALT played the central role, Liechtenstein agreed to follow the Swiss example of lifting secrecy in criminal cases.

One drawback to the country is its inconvenience. No planes fly to Liechtenstein, and even trains rarely stop at little Vaduz, the capital. Zurich, the closest metropolitan area, is a two-hour car ride away.

PERSONAL INCOME TAX: up to 20.8%; non-employed resident aliens may pay 15%.

ESTATE DUTY: 0.5 - 27%

CORPORATE PROFITS TAX: 7.5 - 15%*

CAPITAL GAINS TAX: None

ANNUAL TAX ON CORPORATE CAPITAL: 0.2%

WITHHOLDING TAX: (a) Dividends: 4%

(b) Interest: 4% except short-term deposits or liens.

For tax favored companies, the incorporation or duty on authorized capital is Sfr. 200 plus Sfr. 50 for each additional Sfr. 100,000; also 2% on paid-up capital. The annual tax or registration fee is 0.1% of net worth (min. Sfr. 1,000).

HONG KONG, A GIANT FALTERS: What can one say about Hong Kong? If it weren't for the question of the 1997 treaty deadline, after which sovereignty of virtually the whole country reverts to Red China, there would be no

---

*Not applicable to holding or domiciliary companies.

reservations about it at all. All foreign-source income is exempt from taxes. The country has sophisticated economic and banking systems and a well-developed, strict, banking-secrecy law.

But as long as Britain agrees with China that 365 of the 410 square miles of Hong Kong will rightfully belong to the Peking government in 1997--and there is realistically no choice but to agree--Hong Kong will be to some degree unstable. One shouldn't yet write it off completely, though. It's very doubtful that the Chinese communists would be so stupid as to kill the goose that's given them so many golden eggs. Perhaps some sort of workable accommodation will be reached. But, such an event seems unlikely at the moment.

Some may argue that since the treaty still has over a decade to run, there's no reason not to use Hong Kong as a haven in the meantime. Unfortunately, there are two problems with this logic. First, the very fact that time is running out on the Colony is causing all the best people to try to get out now. Second, it's always a good idea to stay with a particular location, if possible, to build up a relationship with a person or institution there. This can no longer be done using Hong Kong because there is absolutely no certainty about its future.

THE ISLE OF MAN: This 227-square mile island lies in the Irish Sea between Ireland and the U.K. It has many of the same features as the Channel Islands. Personal income and corporate profits taxes are 20%, and there is a one-time incorporation tax for companies (called "associations" here). Although it has exempted itself from the high British value-added tax (VAT), Man is still a sterling bloc country, susceptible to exchange controls if they're ever imposed again.

There are bank-secrecy provisions, however. The Banking Act of 1975 states that the Manx Treasury may inspect a bank's internal records, but this--so far--has only been used to inspect records pertaining to a bank's financial health. And no foreign jurisdiction can gain access to bank-account information. In its short history, this law has resulted in a strict level of bank secrecy. What's more, the island's low-key, conservative atmosphere has enabled it to escape the ire of U.S. tax authorities. Not one tax case has involved the Isle of Man.

There are about 50 banks on the island; most of these are either local or the branches of British banks. Unlike the Channel Islands, Man hasn't many international banks.

Late in 1982 there were a few bankruptcies in the Manx financial sector. Internal control was first tightened, then relaxed again. Through all this turmoil, though, the 1975 secrecy provisions remained unamended.

Communications and services are excellent. Air service is daily from several U.K. cities. Unlike the

Channel Islands, the Isle of Man still welcomes immigrants. The government has set a goal of 75,000 inhabitants. (There are presently some 65,000.) Especially welcome are individuals who are both rich and able to contribute to the cultural betterment of the island.

Man has a double-taxation treaty only with the U.S. While the treaty enables Manx individuals and companies to recover tax credits, and never pay more than 20% taxes, it also provides for full exchange of information between the two tax authorities; that is, to the extent of the Manx law, which provides for confidentiality.

However, the Manx authorities are upset about the way the U.K. has assaulted Manx sovereignty over its bank and tax records. Recently, U.K. tax men tried to invoke the clause of the 1975 U.K. Finance Act stipulating that British emigrants to the Isle of Man must still pay--forever--a tax on income origination in the U.K. But to the relief of Manx authorities, in March 1981, a British High Court ruled that U.K. tax men have no power to investigate Manx bank records, or even force Manx bank branches of British banks to submit to British laws.

In its short tradition as a financial center, the Isle of Man has behaved rather well. It's still tied a bit too much to Britain, and more time is needed to see how it responds to attacks on its financial sovereignty by the superpowers. But so far it earns quite high marks, and perhaps in several more years will be worthy of the big leagues.

Luxembourg, A Second Switzerland?

This tiny Grand Duchy occupies 999 square miles, bordering France, Germany and Belgium. Its population is roughly one-twentieth that of Switzerland. This small size is at once a source of some of Luxembourg's advantages (it's striving to tailor its services to a few better-quality individuals, as does Bermuda) and at the same time, several of its drawbacks (its services are still a bit primitive, and the country continues to be dominated by neighbors Belgium and Germany).

A group of German bankers formed Banque Internationale in 1856, with the aim of creating a laissez-faire center just outside German borders. Since then, Luxembourg has grown into a world financial center. But this growth has been managed cautiously, befitting the general conservatism of the Grand Duchy's citizens. Even with the explosive growth of the past 15 years, only bona fide banks are allowed, no "brass-plate" banks such as are evident in, say, the Caymans. Yet, this rapid growth hasn't strained the infrastructure.

Although 1929 was not a great year in the history of the stock market it was the year in which tiny Luxembourg established its exchange. And on July 31, 1929, the law creating tax-free holding companies was effected, truly putting the country on the haven map.

Much like Austria, Luxembourg can point to a tradition of bank secrecy, implied in Article 458 of the Penal Code. The Bank Act of April 23, 1981 explicitly reinforces this tradition. While the Act does permit information concerning the administration, management, property or ownership of credit institutions to be divulged, customer account secrecy is not threatened by it.

Even though the Grand Duchy shares a common currency with Belgium, the Belgian franc, in almost every other way, it is separate and distinct from its northern neighbor. While Belgium was crippled in the fall of 1983 by a general strike, with all radio, TV, and public services suspended, Luxembourg has not had a strike of any magnitude since 1921. Perhaps the very size of the country is the reason for this apparent cohesiveness; labor leaders, businessmen, and politicians all went to the same schools.

Interest rates tend to be 2-3% lower than those in Luxembourg's three larger neighbors. Unemployment, while a scant 1.7% (approximately 2,200 people) and low by most other countries' standards (except those of Switzerland), is nevertheless at a record high rate and cause for great concern. Paradoxically, the government is happy that it has kept inflation beneath its 10% target level since 1981.

Perhaps this can be excused if one remembers that the Duchy uses the Belgian franc (although it's called the Luxembourg franc), doesn't have a real central bank of its own, and is therefore not entirely responsible for its inflation. In fact, Belgium's price inflation rate last year was 15%.

All is not bright with the fundamentals, however. Like most countries, Luxembourg has long tried to tax and spend its way into prosperity. In general, taxes are very steep. The top rate on personal income tax is 57%; on estates, 48%. The corporate profits tax is 40%. The banks pay lower rates because of tradition and because they are large revenue generators. Economic output shrank by nearly 2% last year, although the banking sector had huge profits.

The government knows it has a good thing in the banks. They employ 8% of the work force and contribute 30% of the Duchy's fiscal income. Not surprisingly, the constitutional monarchy wants to help its banks. How often does a country's Finance Minister say this about his nation's banks: "The political authorities are fully conscious of the fact that the tax system is not as attractive to the banks as it could be in comparison with other centers."

Taxes on banks were, in effect, reduced recently when the government lifted the levies due from profits on exchange-rate gains. Officials are absolutely opposed to any turnover or sales taxes on gold trading; taxes which even Switzerland has. They also are considering applying the same tax-free status to silver trading. Interest-withholding taxes, at 5%, are less that those of Austria or Switzerland.

Luxembourg has about 5,500 holding companies, the centerpiece of the country's financial attraction. These firms can invest money worldwide and pay neither taxes on profits nor withholding taxes on interest and dividends; they pay only an annual registration fee of 0.2% of shareholder's equity.

Of equal or greater interest are the fiduciary accounts that Luxembourg's banks are now emphasizing. It is for wealthier, tax-shy individuals that Luxembourg has begun shifting its emphasis away from wholesale banking toward the retail market.

Wholesale banking consists of banking (buying) deposits on the interbank market and loaning them out to other institutions, relying on a fractional interest-rate mark-up for profit. It was probably the Luxembourg banks' unusually large concentration of bad loans to eastern Europe and Latin America that spurred them into the retail market.

These institutions have turned to private banking to cater to the needs of high-net worth (say, over U.S. $250,000) individuals because advisory and custodial fees, as well as trading commissions, mean big profits. The banks hope to attract clients from Switzerland by offering lower commissions and a generally lower-profile banking center.

Try as they may to switch to private, "fiduciary" accounts, Luxembourg's banks have not been very successful. Fully 85.6% of their deposits come from other banks, and that figure has held steady through the recent past.

There are good reasons for this. Granted, bankers in Luxembourg "talk excitedly about establishing private entrances and plush reception rooms for wealthy clients to avoid the bustle of the public banking hall." But these are superficial trimmings mixed with a touch of grandiosity. For, in reality, it is the Swiss who have been successful at attracting wealthy individuals. Compared with their Swiss counterparts, the Luxembourg banks seem, by and large, to be rather amateurish with no tradition of portfolio management (not that the Swiss banks have a great track record on that score). Talent in general has to be imported from elsewhere. Futhermore, portfolio managers at the Luxembourg banks don't have the sophisticated computer tools that can be found in Zurich and Geneva. Reading their banks' literature usually makes one think of a parvenu--long on enthusiasm but short on tradition and the "feel" for the hard-asset, low-tax philosophy found at the best Swiss banks. There's a lot of potential in Luxembourg, but it hasn't yet been realized.

While both the country and its banks offer some attractive features to the investor, there are drawbacks to Luxembourg as a haven.

Luxembourg has an economic and monetary union with Belgium (which is deeply in debt) has a weak currency, and is crippled by strikes. The Duchy is also a member of the EC, the Common Market; a fact that has caused difficulties at times. In 1978, the EC issued its "fourth company law" designed to force greater disclosure from all member-country companies. After an intense struggle, Luxembourg got most of its holding companies exempted from this law. However, the country did pledge to alter its holding-company laws to provide, as of 1990, a public listing of shareholders.

This doesn't mean Luxembourg will necessarily keep this pledge. It has largely ignored those parts of the 1978 EC directive to which it objected. As a result, the EC is about to begin infringement proceedings. Common Market officials are upset with Luxembourg and have put this question to the Duchy: "Where is the harm in increasing transparency for holding companies?" But apparently they have never gotten a satisfactory reply. "They seem to think that if we touch one element in the economic edifice, then the whole pack of cards will fall to the ground."

Unfortunately, that is exactly what would happen. Much of the reason for investment in Luxembourg would vanish. If this harassment continues, sooner or later the Duchy may have to choose between its haven status and EC membership. An educated guess is that it will hold firm on its privacy laws. After all, Luxembourg's national motto is _Mir wole bleiwe wat mir sin_--we want to stay the way we are.

BAD LOAN EXPOSURE: Unfortunately, the Duchy has a startlingly high proportion of loans to eastern European and Latin American countries on its banks' books. As of the third quarter of 1982, loans to these two regions totaled around $98 billion; that is, Luxembourg's banks held between 15% and 20% of _all_ loans to these two areas. Latin loans were $64 billion (9.4% of total bank assets) while loans to eastern Europe amounted to $34 billion (5.8%).

In terms of physical safety, Luxembourg is much more vulnerable to invasion than Fortress Switzerland--it's been invaded no less than 22 times in the past two centuries, an average of once a decade. Steep domestic taxes and social welfare spending have already been mentioned. And ARBED, Europe's fourth largest steel plant and formerly Luxembourg's pride, its largest corporation, is now near bankruptcy. This could adversely affect local banks, which still carry loans to the company as assets on their books.

SUMMARY OF TAXES

PERSONAL INCOME TAX: Up to 57%

ESTATE DUTY: 2 - 48%

CORPORATE PROFITS TAX: 40%

CAPITAL GAINS TAX: Taxed on income or profits**

ANNUAL TAX ON CORPORATE CAPITAL: 0.5%

WITHHOLDING TAX: (a) dividends 15% (2.5 -10%)***

(b) interest 5%

TAX FAVORED COMPANIES: (a) incorporation tax or duty on authorized capital 1%

(b) annual tax or registration fee 0.2% of issued capital

DOUBLE TAXATION TREATIES:**Austria, Belgium, Brazil, Denmark, Finland, France, Germany, Ireland, Italy, Netherlands, U.K., U.S.A.

Singapore, Waiting in the Wings?

Assuming that the British, as expected, turn Hong Kong over to the Chinese, it's an open question whether Singapore can actually replace the former colony. Political freedom is a necessary prerequisite of any country that wants a stable, free financial and economic system. Unfortunately, Singapore has many aspects of a dictatorship, albeit a fairly benevolent one.

**Not applicable to holding or domiciliary companies.

***Treaty Rates.

Nevertheless, it is a land of tremendous energy and, unencumbered by the nagging doubts afflicting Hong Kong, Singapore gives the impression that it is capable of accomplishing anything it sets out to do.

Singapore has already surpassed Hong Kong as an offshore banking center. But until fall-1983, fees earned by its banks for investment management services and advice were taxed at 40%. Almost immediately after Hong Kong's troubles became well publicized, the tax was reduced to 10%. Simultaneously, the 40% income tax that had been paid by non-residents investing off-shore funds in off-shore markets was abolished.

So, one of the two hindrances to Singapore's haven development was quickly removed. The second hindrance, however, will be more difficult to obviate. This hindrance revolves around Singapore's laws concerning client's liabilities. In fact, in 1983, Morgan Grenfell became so concerned about the client liability question that it pulled its off-shore Asian Investment Fund out and transferred it to the un-Asian island of Jersey.

For instance, while Singapore does have legal provisions to protect bank secrecy, there is still no specific, unambiguous Swiss-style law. Whether a government that is used to handing down somewhat arbitrary edicts concerning personal freedom will necessarily have trouble handing down clear laws regarding financial freedom, is a question that warrants thought.

Panama

"In ten years much of the European and Western world's criminal money will reside in Panama," The Use of Offshore Banks and Companies.

In Panama the U.S. government faces a particularly tough situation. The country is one of Washington's closest Latin allies, and is located in such a vitally strategic area that to antagonize Panama would obviously be detrimental to U.S. foreign policy.

But this same ally, faced with an unemployment rate of over 20%, sees its salvation in the further encouragement of its one "growth industry": a financial center with the strictest bank-secrecy laws in the Western Hemisphere. Furthermore, the corrupt military leadership doesn't do much to hide the fact that drug money is a mainstay of both the Panamanian economy and its own income. To gauge the extent of this, in 1985 about $2.1 billion in cash was exported from Panamanian banks to the U.S. Federal Reserve for deposit or transfer. Moreover, much of this tremendous amount was denominated in twenty dollar bills, which are commonly used in drug dealings. This "surplus cash" thus exported can only represent a part of Panamanian drug money.

Since anyone can run money into Panama in complete secrecy, and since so much of this is drug money (which, politically, is a good deal more unpopular in the U.S. than tax-evasion money), the questionable source of these funds has raised Washington's ire. While Panama is an important U.S. ally, there are recent signs that even conservative anti-communists are getting fed up with the situation. In June 1986, Senator Jesse Helms called Panamanian strongman General Manuel Antonio Noriega "the head of the biggest drug-trafficking organization in the Western Hemisphere." There are also allegations that Noriega was involved in the deaths of two recent Panamanian presidents.

Panama's bank-secrecy strictures are found in its Law on Coded Bank Accounts. Anyone who breaches secrecy is liable to a maximum six month prison sentence and a $10,000 fine.

But this is just the start of Panamanian-style secrecy, for bank accounts are usually opened and operated by companies formed by depositors. These are "paper" companies, formed by local lawyers for fees ranging from $600 to $1,500, with annual maintenance fees of $250. Actual owners of these companies need not identify themselves. They can appoint "nominee directors," often the local lawyers. In brief, Panama offers two tiers of secrecy: a registered company with anonymous owners depositing funds in an anonymous bank account.

In practice, it is virtually impossible to get information about these registered companies. Not even the Panamanian government knows exactly how many of them exist. Foreign governments can show that a company's funds are profits from the most revolting child prostitution ring, but the Ministry of Commerce, responsible for following up on these allegations, will take no action and provide no information unless the alleged crime not only is a crime in Panama but has also been committed in Panama. This goes one step further than either the Cayman Islands or Switzerland, which will give information only when the alleged crime is also a crime in that particular country (In both countries drug trafficking and child prostitution are illegal; tax evasion is not.)

Consistent with this line, Panamanian authorities will take steps to curtail drug trafficking in Panama (U.S. Coast Guard ships are allowed to board and search Panamanian vessels suspected of transporting drugs with prior notification to Panama's government). But drug-trade profits, once in the banking system, are inviolate.

There has, in fact, been only one recorded case in which U.S. law enforcement requests resulted in disclosure. This was in the heinous Jonestown, Guyana massacre case; apparently a crime and an organization too revolting even for the soldiers/policemen in de facto control of Panama.

THE NATIONAL GUARD

The center of power in Panama is the National Guard. Even when the titular President is a civilian, it's a well known fact that nothing of substance can be successfully undertaken without National Guard assistance or acquiescence. It's also common knowledge that the Guard is riddled with corruption, and will turn over criminals to foreign authorities only if the criminal is foolish enough not to have paid his "dues" to the National Guard.

The list of activities in which the Guard is involved is long. It provides safe passage for smugglers (or arms, drugs or other contraband) and spies to and from North and South America and Cuba. It is the Guard against which U.S. investigators are pitted. When presented with evidence of bank accounts holding drug profits (which is what happened in the Justice Department's undercover "Operation Swordfish" in October 1982), National Guard officers claim (as they did then) that their hands are tied: "If the Panamanian government asks a Panama bank how much is in a secret account, the bank officer would be within his rights to deny such information."

As mentioned before, the Guard either installs or supports each civilian president. And it's interesting to note that Panama's only recently elected president was a partner in a major law firm which is very active in registering off-shore companies. This shows how intimately the Panamanian establishment is connected to the banking laws.

There are about 3,000 local lawyers in Panama. Unfortunately there is neither a code of ethics nor any internal disciplinary mechanism. Most lawyers ask no questions when forming companies and cannot be held responsible if anyone is defrauded. Small wonder, therefore, that the saying, "it is a rare lawyer who does not cheat his client" is common. But it seems the client is willing to put up with corruption in order to secure his affairs.

There are currently 136 banks in Panama. Contrary to what one would expect, these are bona fide banks--not the "brass-plate banks" usually found in the Caribbean. Panama had a brass-plate system in the 1960's. However, when two spectacular failures occurred, eligibility was tightened. To be licensed now, not only does a bank need $250,000 in capital and a physical presence, but only major international banks with headquarters in "responsible" foreign nations are allowed to operate inside the country. Panama knows well what type of characters usually operate out of Caribbean bank havens. (Indeed, it takes one to know one.) So, applications are given to the headquarter offices of banks in the U.S., the U.K., France, Switzerland, Japan, etc. Rejections are not uncommon, especially for, say, Bahamian-based banks wanting a

Panamanian subsidiary or for an American subsidiary in the Bahamas wanting to open its own subsidiary in Panama.

So, Panama's set-up is air-tight: anonymous companies with secret accounts in banks with little danger of going bankrupt. Further strengthening Panama's position is the fact that it has important ties to the U.S. Although the Canal is no longer U.S. property, operating and defending it is still a U.S. responsibility and will remain so for the rest of this century. In addition, while Panama officially has its own currency, the balboa, this is closely tied to the U.S. dollar on a par basis (one balboa equals one dollar). Indeed, U.S. currency is legal tender throughout Panama.

For other obvious reasons Washington doesn't want to antagonize Panama. It is quite cognizant of the fact that even reputable lawyers and bankers claim that any American pressures for change will be poorly greeted. Banking is Panama's only real industry. Its agricultural base is stagnating; it has few natural resources and an expensive labor force. The financial sector accounts for 9% of the GNP and is growing at a 22% rate per year. Total assets in Panamanian banks are an estimated (early 1983) $38 billion, about the same amount as those in the Cayman banks.

The Panamanian situation leaves the U.S. government with no happy alternatives. It has tried to influence Panama to reform itself in minor "step-by-step" ways. Thus far, however, Panama's behavior hasn't much changed. As the recent U.S. tide of discontent with General Noriega comes on the heels of the Marcos and Duvalier affairs, one wonders whether the U.S. will not take a more activist stance in Panamanian politics.

Aside from its secrecy status, Panama has certain tax-haven features. It is common knowledge that many people use this haven and are quite happy with it. However, the facts argue persuasively that Panama probably does not represent a viable alternative because the attitude of the Panamanian powers is simply too tinged with corruption. Authorities who not only turn a blind eye to fraud but actually abet it (in return for a piece of the action) are not individuals to whom one should entrust money.

If one were a drug trafficker or white slaver, one would of course feel safer in Panama than in Switzerland or Austria, which would certainly aid any prosecuting government. But it is because these countries are not corrupt that they are preferable to Panama.

The Cayman Islands

The Cayman Islands is a stable, rich and tax free Caribbean nation with no political parties, no unemployment, and no racial tension. It also has--or has had until recently--very strict bank secrecy laws.

The effect of this law, the Confidential Relationships (Preservation) Law, has transformed the small Cayman Islands into one of the foremost financial centers in the world. There are now as many banks represented in George Town, the capital, as there are days of the year.

Not only is it a criminal offense, under the Confidential Relationships Law, for a bank employee to divulge any information which has not been authorized by the customer, but one can be jailed for even making the inquiry. This goes a step beyond even Swiss law. Any bank employee giving such information is liable "to a fine not exceeding $5,000 or to imprisonment for a term not exceeding 2 years, or both." Needless to say, anyone so convicted--or even suspected--of breaching bank secrecy would almost certainly be fired from the bank, and would find no others to take him, as Caymanian banks are necessarily jealous of their reputations. To the author's knowledge, no bank employee has been charged with this crime.

There is an Inspector of Banks, appointed by the Governor. This Inspector can, and does, regularly check the books of all banks to insure no impropriety. However, he is not allowed access to the accounts themselves or to information about a depositor, except by court order, when the account holder is suspected of a crime. In this regard, Caymanian law is similar to Swiss law.

Caymanian banking laws also resemble their Swiss counterparts in areas other than stringent secrecy. Bank accounts can be opened in _any_ currency that the depositor wishes to use. Banks can also open accounts for gold and silver, both for buying and selling. And while banks cannot trade securities for the depositor, trusts can.

All these points aside, the Cayman Islands has one major drawback which cannot be ignored. While it has the strictest laws of the English speaking world, use of the Islands' banks is not recommended because the U.S. tax authorities are infuriated by them, and the country itself is of no strategic importance to Washington. If the U.S. government ever decided to crack down hard on the havens, the Cayman Islands would probably be at the top of the "bad-guy" list. Panama, Luxembourg, Liechtenstein, Switzerland and Austria are all nations with strict secrecy laws. But these nations have other things going for them that would prevent Washington from cracking down too hard. Unfortunately, the Caymans do not share this advantage.

This point was just recently underscored: On July 3, 1986, a landmark treaty was signed between the Caymans and the U.S.; a treaty which could change not only the Caymans but the other Caribbean havens as well. From the _Wall Street Journal_ of July 3, 1986:

> "The government of the tiny Caribbean islands has agreed to open up financial records and to cooperate in other ways with Justice Department

> prosecutors in most types of criminal investigations ranging from mail fraud and corrupt activities by federal contractors to insider-trading cases.
>
> U.S. officials hope that the agreement hammered out during more than a year of negotiations, will serve as a model for mutual legal assistance treaties currently under discussion with other off-shore banking centers, including the Bahamas, the British Virgin Islands, and the Turks and Caicos Islands. The treaty with the Caymans will be the first such sweeping law enforcement agreement involving the Caribbean basin. By making the Caymans more attractive to legitimate off-shore investment, the treaty is expected to increase pressure on neighboring countries to ease their bank-secrecy laws . . .
>
> The treaty appears to be part of a new strategy by officials of the islands to develop tourism and promote growth of their banking and insurance industries. The islands hired Bray & Co., a politically connected Washington lobbying firm, to try to spruce up their image and encourage legitimate American investment. Now that the Caymans have agreed to sign the treaty, 'they can become legitimate,' says Robert Breier, a Miami tax attorney . . .
>
> Since the 1960s, island officials have balked at providing any information to help U.S. authorities pursue tax evaders; and on the surface, at least, the treaty allows them to adhere to that principle. Bank records or other information turned over by the Cayman Islands, for example, can't be used to file criminal tax charges against any individual or company in the U.S.
>
> But when prosecutors suspect that violations of other laws are connected to alleged tax violations, the treaty calls for providing speedy access to the relevant bank records. 'We can package the case under a different statute and still get the same information,' said one Justice Department official."

It remains to be seen whether the U.S. can bring charges against those who have only evaded taxes, but when the U.S. government has so "packaged" its case, that information in question should be forthcoming.

The important thing here is that such a treaty was inevitable. Any jurisdiction which is so dependent on the U.S. for trade cannot hope to be able to protect its sovereignty.

Chapter 9

Getting Wealth Overseas (and Getting It Back)

Even though the doors are closing, there still are completely legal, non-reportable methods to turn money in the U.S. into money in a safe foreign jurisdiction. In this section, these methods will be explored.

POSTAL MONEY ORDERS

One problem facing any American who wishes to transfer funds overseas is the potential availability of the transfer records to the unauthorized scrutiny of others.

Fortunately, there are ways to safe-guard against unwanted intrusions on one's privacy. An account holder can arrange his affairs so that a maximum of confidentiality can be maintained, both in depositing and withdrawing funds.

For instance, in the United States, one can go to any of the thousands of U.S. post offices and get a postal money order. These money orders are purchased for cash. The money order offers complete confidentiality because no questions are asked concerning the identities of the payee and the payer. The money order is blank except for the amount paid. One can complete the form in any way one pleases. On the line marked "purchaser," one can scribble in any word or leave it blank. The purchaser may even want to use that particular post office's number, putting it down as the "sender." Then, only the check's destination need be filled in. To do this, one can just use the name of a bank, or even a person at that bank. In any case, there are no records of the person who sent the check.

In the past, this device had limited application because the maximum allowable amount on a postal money order was only U.S. $250. In a recent change, however, that maximum has been raised to U.S. $500. There are no limits on the number of postal money orders that one can send, but it would probably be prudent to spread one's purchases out over several post offices. This is especially easy, of course, if one lives in a metropolitan area.

MONEY ORDERS

Aside of the post office, there are other establishments at which one can purchase checks privately. Some supermarkets around the country (e.g. Safeway) offer money orders. The limits on these types of checks are usually smaller than those at the post office; typically $100. But, the opportunity is worth exploring.

The more urban areas of the country (e.g., New York, Chicago) are rife with businesses called "currency exchanges." These are often referred to as "poor man's banks," so don't expect to buy Swiss francs here. Currency exchanges acquired this nickname because of their locations (generally in poorer parts of cities) and the fact that many distribute food stamps and welfare checks (also cashing the latter).

Recently, however, many exchanges have added credit card cash dispensaries and are branching out into the suburbs. All exchanges, though, offer the same type of money orders for cash that the post office sells. The current rate charged is $1 for every $100 of face value. Maximum check amounts vary among the different exchanges; indeed, some have no limits at all.

Generally, these maximums tend to be small but, again, a continuous program of, say $100 per day adds up to $36,000 per year or $360,000 over 10 years.

However, there is a method for turning dollars in this country into Swiss-held precious metals with no reporting requirements. In the next section, this intriguing system will be explored more closely.

PRIVATE METALS TRANSFER TO SWITZERLAND

The author believes that precious metals should generally be bought outright, rather than in the form of futures or options. A portion of one's total holdings should be under the owner's direct control, stored either on one's property or in a safety-deposit box. However, the author believes that part of everyone's metals holdings should be in Switzerland, as protection against possible actions by their governments.

Growing regulations on the overseas transfer of funds have made it increasingly difficult for investors to hold precious metals abroad. Nevertheless, there is an innovative, fast, safe way to write a check to one's local bank or broker--or even just pick up the phone--for bullion or coins that one owns and stores in Zurich. Using this method, it is also possible to avoid any reporting requirement, even if one buys $100 million worth of Swiss gold. By the same token, this method is equally useful for amounts less than $1,000.

The generic term for the device one uses is "preferred non-fungible warehouse receipt." It is important to note that there is a significant distinction between "fungible" and "non-fungible" warehouse receipts. FUNGIBLE means that one's silver and gold are stored in bulk along with that of everyone else. One cannot point to a specific coin or bar and say: "That's mine." NON-FUNGIBLE means that one's silver and gold are kept separate from that of everyone else, often labeled with the owner's name. If the storage company goes bankrupt and one's metal is stored using fungible receipts, one may have to wait for the courts to go through lengthy accounting procedures before ownership of the metals is finally determined.

Four issuers of preferred non-fungible warehouse receipts that immediately come to mind are: Mocatta Metals; Manfra, Tordella and Brookes; Brooks Armoured Car Service; and North American Depository. Mocatta's brand new "Delivery Order" is the best of these, so it will be discussed here. The other services offer delivery only in the U.S., particularly in Delaware for the tax advantages. But Mocatta offers delivery in Delaware, as well as in Zurich, and this is what makes it superior.

Available since 1981, Mocatta's Delivery Order made its debut in a period of declining metal prices. As a result, it's generally been overlooked. However, since prices should be rising again in the next few years, it behooves investors to acquaint themselves with this innovation.

Mocatta does not operate as a coin or metals dealer on the retail level. Rather, it is one of the sources that coin and metals dealers use to get their wares. The company is a dealer's dealer, as well as a broker's broker. Thus, Mocatta's Delivery Orders are not available to the public directly. Rather, they are offered through participating brokers and banks on a commission basis.

Beginning with the basics, it has become more and more evident that one should have specific coins or bars set aside only for oneself. Given the recent flurry of big bankruptcies among coin companies, this point cannot be overemphasized. Under the various sets of circumstances in which an individual might want an institution to store his gold in exchange for a paper receipt (say, for convenience or international diversification), it's safest when that receipt represents a claim on an actual piece of metal with "one's name on it". This is particularly important when dealing with a non-bank institution. A good Swiss bank with virtually no loans, except to its clients to enable them to buy metals--like Foreign Commerce Bank of Zurich--is perhaps the safest place to store gold without "one's name on it." But coin dealers or even brokerage houses are not such safe bets.

Everyone has seen the messes created by some coin dealers who offer to "store" their clients' gold--indeed sometimes there is no gold and one's money is used to buy corporate jets.

The big stock brokerage houses that offer gold certificates are certainly far less likely to defraud their customers. But one must realize that, in most cases, there is no specific portion of metal with one's name on it. The majority of the paper receipts, issued by institutions acting as gold warehouses, are not fully backed by gold. In this respect, they bear ironic resemblance to the old paper-money receipts of national treasuries; receipts which the public was assured could be exchanged for gold on demand--although there was never a sufficient supply of the metal to satisfy all claims at once.

What Mocatta offers is the exception to this rule. When one buys a Delivery Order, the purchaser is buying a specific portion of gold set aside for him in Switzerland at MAT Securitas Express Ltd. of Zurich, one of Europe's largest precious metals warehousers and transporters. MAT stores all its gold and silver in the Duty Free Zone at the Zurich Airport. (The gold can also be stored at the Wilmington Trust Company of Delaware, although this has to be specifically requested. Not surprisingly, most people find the Swiss option more attractive, especially as there are no reporting requirements. Technically, no money leaves the U.S. The Order is transferable so one can sell or give it to anyone. One can also physically claim the gold, or have it transferred elsewhere.

The gold delivered in Switzerland through Mocatta is there for its owner to examine. One simply has to make an appointment, present a Delivery Order and, as the owner, is allowed to inspect it. The number on one's order will match the number on the stored gold.

AS SAFELY AS HUMANLY POSSIBLE

Mocatta goes to great lengths to assure its clients that the viability of these Delivery Orders does not depend on the health or the honesty of either MAT Securitas or

Mocatta itself. One owns the gold one buys; in the event of either company's insolvency, the gold is completely safe from confiscation by creditors.

When one buys the Order, Mocatta pledges that the amount of gold it represents corresponds precisely to the amount kept in storage for the purchaser. Furthermore, the entire transaction is insured by Lloyds of London against every possible loss except war and government confiscation. Since these are less likely to happen in Switzerland than in any other country, one's gold is about as safe as is humanly possible.

Mocatta has had this coverage with Lloyds on an annually renewable basis for many years now. Of course, there is no guarantee that Mocatta will always renew. However, at present, the company says that it has no intention of changing this policy. If Mocatta were to do so, it makes the following pledge: If Mocatta cancels the Lloyds policy (renewable each January 28), it will take out ads to that effect in both the <u>Wall Street Journal</u> and <u>Financial Times</u> 30 days before the policy expires (about the end of December). In addition, Mocatta will mail an announcement letter to anyone who has left an address with the company in New York.

A WAY AROUND THE REPORTING REQUIREMENTS

It is quite likely that U.S. exchange controls will eventually be imposed. Already the mechanism is in place: any transfer of $10,000 in monetary instruments overseas must be registered with the U.S. government. (Canadians are still free of any reporting requirements.) Thus, it is illegal for an American to use a check to buy $10,000 worth of gold at a Swiss bank without notifying his government.

The Mocatta Delivery Order, however, skirts this requirement: no monetary instrument leaves the country, at least not from the gold purchaser. This purchaser merely makes his check out to his local bank or broker, who is empowered to sell the Orders to the public. And, if one deals with Benham metals through an affiliated money market fund (Capital Preservation Fund), one doesn't even have to write a check, just have funds transferred from one account to another.

Granted, the Delivery Order itself must be transferred in some way to MAT Securities in Zurich before the gold can be claimed. Legally, Delivery Orders are "assignable, non-negotiable" documents of title. As they are assignable, the owner can transfer title to anyone. But being non-negotiable, their overseas transfer should not be subject to the reporting requirements of the Bank Secrecy Act. Under that law, only cash, traveller's checks, money order to bearer-form negotiable securities, (like some stocks and bonds, must be reported.)

In short, the author believes that the Orders are far and away the best and most private legal method available to transfer funds overseas for safe purchase of precious metals. (Indeed, it is an open question as to how long the U.S. government will allow this avenue to remain open. Jim Stucky, head Delivery-Order trader for C. Rhyne & Associates in Seattle, told the author that it is probable that this loophole may be closed in two years, if the Orders gain in popularity.

WHERE TO BUY MOCATTA DELIVERY ORDERS

Mocatta doesn't market its Delivery Orders directly to the public. Instead, they are sold to banks and brokers who then sell them to the public.

There are probably only four companies experienced in handling these Orders: International Trading Group, Ltd. (ITG), C. Rhyne & Associates, Western Federal Corporation, and Benham Certified Metals.

Of these, the author favors Benham and Rhyne. ITG has a reputation for bad service; slick, pushy salespeople; and high prices.

Western Federal offers the orders but does not encourage them.

Rhyne is a well-respected coin and bullion dealer and has been in business since 1975. Its address is: C. Rhyne & Associates, 110 Cherry Street, Seattle, WA 98104, (800) 426-7835. Ask for Jim Stucky or Craig Rhyne.

Benham is one of the best--and least expensive--bullion and coin dealers. It is also affiliated with the Capital Preservation Fund, a money market fund that invests only in safe T-bills. The Capital Preservation Fund is a perfect way to safely "store" liquid cash, and it also makes buying a Delivery Order very easy. In fact, this company strives to make all its services easier and the author has been a happy client since 1978. Address: 755 Page Mill Rd., Palo Alto, CA 94304 (800) 447- 4653.

THE FULL COST

Mocatta sells gold in units. The minimum order is one unit with no half unit sales allowed. Units are in gold and silver bars of various sizes, and in coins. The unit quantities and minimum order amounts are shown in Table I. In dollar terms, the minimum order is 20 one-ounce coins. If Krugerrands are selling at $350 apiece, the unit of twenty will sell at a $7,000 base price.

When one purchases a Delivery Order, the bank or broker will ask that a check for the full purchase price be sent immediately. (Benham customers associated with the Capital Preservation Fund can just allow their accounts to be debited). For those purchasing coin rolls, the matter is simple. But if one buys bars, be aware that until the Delivery Order is issued, the amount one wants to buy is reckoned, for price calculations, in exact kilograms (32.15 troy ounces). Then, when the specific Order is allocated and the actual gold purchased, there may be adjustments in the exact weight of the bar one ends up with, as a result of occasional slight variations in bar weight. Any price adjustment will usually be less than 3% in either direction.

Here again, Benham Metals tries to make things easier for the purchaser. One can immediately lock in exact prices for every size of bar, except silver 1,000 oz. bars. The company tries to locate the exact size bar and get back to the client with the exact price within half an hour.

TABLE I: MOCATTA'S MINIMUM ORDERS

One Unit Equals

GOLD

1	One-Kg bar (32.15 troy ounces)	minimum order one unit
1	100-oz bar	minimum order one unit
1	400-oz bar	minimum order one unit
20	One-oz Krugerrands*	minimum order one unit
20	One-oz Canadian Maple Leafs*	minimum order one unit

GOLD (minimum order 10 units)

20	Austrian 100 Coronas**	minimum order ten units
20	Mexican 50 Pesos*	minimum order ten units

SILVER

1 1,000-oz bar	minimum order ten units
1 bag of coins, $1,000	minimum order ten units

*Stored in a numbered, sealed tube.
**Because of lowest premiums, this coin gives you the most gold for your money as of 9/1/86.

ISSUANCE AND STORAGE FEES

There are also issuance and storage fees that must be included in a Mocatta Delivery Order. The issuance charge for the order itself is $100, regardless of the number of units.

In addition, MAT Securitas, the metals warehouse, charges storage fees based on the London P.M. fix of the gold's value on the day before the Order payment is made. MAT charges one half of 1% annually, prorated from the time one buys to December 31 of that year. The charge is, then, one half of 1% for the first five calendar years, and 2% a year for each succeeding year thereafter. (As will be discussed later, there's really no reason to store at MAT Securitas for as long as five years.) The yearly charge is based on gold's price on December 12th of the preceding year. Storage is paid by buying stamps to be put on the reverse of the Delivery Order. The annual storage check, like all payments from the customer, is made out to Mocatta Metals in New York. If one fails to pay the storage fees for five years, MAT Securitas will sell the gold, pay the outstanding fees, and put the remaining funds in a non-interest-bearing account until the Delivery Order is surrendered.

COMMISSIONS

To the $100 issuance charge and the storage fees must be added the bank or broker's fee. Sometimes this is in the form of a commission; sometimes in the form of a fixed mark-up in the gold price. In addition, commissions vary, often depending on the amounts purchased.

International Trading Group's normal commission rate is 3%. For orders over $100,000, the rate falls to 2%. On one-million-dollar orders, ITG's commission can drop to 1%.

C. Rhyne's highest charge is 2 3/4%. At an order amount of $355,000, the 1 1/4% commission-rate threshold is reached. Regardless of the amount, Rhyne's fees do not drop below 1%.

Benham's charges are a flat 1% regardless of the amount bought. For the author, Benham is the all-around best broker with which to deal. The company is able to keep its charges so low because its prime focus is to get people to invest in its money market funds. Given the ease with which its money market clients can purchase the Orders, there is, indeed, good reason to make use of the company's funds.

ONCE IN SWITZERLAND, WHAT THEM?

At some point, one may want to have one's gold or silver transferred to a Swiss bank. In fact, since the MAT Securitas storage charge increases to 2% per year after five years, one should plan on transferring the gold to one's own bank. This is very easy, being essentially a bookkeeping procedure. In fact, to avoid the 6.2% Swiss turnover tax on precious metals, both MAT Securitas and one's Swiss bank may well store their gold at the same Duty-free Zone at the Zurich Airport. If this is the case, shipping charges will be minuscule.

Keep in mind that if the owner wants to keep his gold segregated after it has been transferred from MAT to his own Swiss bank, storage costs could well run double or triple what they would have been if the metals were allowed to be commingled with other clients' holdings.

If one is dealing with a reputable Swiss bank like the Foreign Commerce Bank of Zurich, however, safety shouldn't be an issue. The fact that this bank is over 100% liquid means that it is in no danger of insolvency. The name of this bank comes up because it is one of the two Swiss banks that store both gold and silver in the client's name, i.e., off the bank's balance sheet in its own space at the Duty Free Zone. The other bank is Cambio and Valorenbank (P.O. 535 8021 Zurich). Its account opening minimum is $50,000, as opposed to Foco's $10,000.

In any case, should one want one's Delivery Order metal transferred to another bank, simply inform the bank currently holding the gold, and it will make all the necessary arrangements. One should also ask the bank how to send the actual Delivery Order certificates.

There are other options aside of transferring the metal to one's bank. Of course, one can claim one's gold by the unit and pick it up at the MAT offices (Sihfeldstrasses 88 in Zurich) simply by presenting the Delivery Order.

MAT will also ship the metals to any location that one specifies. The owner pays for the shipping, which MAT arranges at the cost of $20 per unit out-charge. However, before MAT will ship one's property, it requires proof that the signature on the Order, instructing the company to ship, is authentic. It will accept the same signature guarantees that North American banks and brokerage houses make available to their clients. If the owner wants to transfer the metals to his Swiss bank, the bank will make certain that the necessary paperwork is completed.

A BUY-BACK POLICY

Although Mocatta doesn't always guarantee to buy back, it does currently have a buy-back policy on its products. If one has the Order certificate and decides for some reason to sell it, one can simply take it to either Mocatta or the broker through whom it was bought originally and either one will pay the owner the current market value of the metals. (Actually, if the Order is returned to the broker, he will send it on to Mocatta in New York for processing. Turnaround time for this is about seven days.)

As mentioned earlier, it can take as long as two months after the purchase date to actually receive the Delivery Order certificate issued by MAT. If, for any reason, one wants to sell before receiving the Order, it is possible to redeem one's cash, minus the broker's commission and Mocatta's $100 issuance charge. If one wishes to sell, however, it is necessary to physically deliver the Order Confirmation, which the broker sends to the owner, Mocatta Metals offices, at 4 World Trade Center, Suite 5200, New York City.

If one owns gold in the U.S. and wants to transfer it to Switzerland using the Mocatta Order, it is possible--but only if one is willing to pay vastly higher shipping and handling costs. Indeed, anyone who plans to use this method might as well arrange for the physical transport of the metals personally--the cost would be comparable. It is much cheaper and easier, instead, to sell the metals here and use the funds generated to buy Orders. Mocatta's shipping costs are low: only rarely are metals physically delivered from the U.S. to Zurich. The usual procedure is for Mocatta to transfer gold or silver from its affiliates closer to Zurich--some, perhaps, only yards away--to the metals new home under the auspices of MAT.

Finally, if a Delivery Order is lost or destroyed, MAT will issue the owner another one; however, the cost is now low. One has to put up either an indemnity bond for twice the then-prevailing market value of the metals or an open-ended indemnity bond. Both are expensive and sometimes difficult to obtain. Delivery Orders, on the other hand, are inexpensive and easy to get, if one's purpose is to transfer metals to Zurich without violating any government reporting laws.

DIAMONDS

It is commonly reported that one of the few remaining ways to privately transform and transfer wealth is in the form of gemstones and diamonds. It is believed that one need only know the wholesale prices of these stones in order to be able to effectively transfer their value overseas. And while the finest quality emeralds, rubies and sapphires can be just as expensive as diamonds, on a per carat basis, diamonds are better simply because most people aren't able to judge the wholesale prices of the colored gemstones. To avoid being duped in gemstones, then, one needs a much more thorough understanding of the market than with diamonds. One of the best ways to become well acquainted with the buying and selling of diamonds and other colored stones is to read David Marcum's highly acclaimed book, The Dow Jones-Irwing Guide to Fine Gems and Jewelry, available in most book stores in the U.S. and Canada.

Diamonds can be purchased with cash, as was formerly more common with coins. Perhaps this state of affairs still exists in the diamond industry because it is more closed, even clannish, than the retail coin industry.

To make matters easier for the average person, one can buy, attached to one's gemstone, a G.I.A. (Gemological Institute of America) diamond grading report which makes clear the quality, and by implication, the value of what one has acquired.

Even so, if a diamond is bought in New York and taken to, say, Zurich to be sold, the investor will lose at least 5%, and as much as 20%, on the spreads between his buying and selling price--and that's if the investor pays the proper wholesale price. But, for the individual who wants to get a lot of money out of the country quickly, even a 20% loss of value may well be worth the price. Indeed, one of the author's friends in the diamond industry has a South African client who claims he'll accept a 90% loss on his diamond sales if it means that he can get enough money out of South Africa to live on for the first year and/or enough money to get started again should he ever feel the need to leave his native land.

Each person's "emergency needs" differ, but whatever these needs are, it should only take a small number of diamonds to satisfy most of them. For example, one million dollars worth of diamonds can fit in a matchbox. Even if one loses 25% of their sale, when the diamonds go on auction at Sotheby's or Christie's in Zurich, one still has a fairly substantial sum of money remaining.

Only time will tell if the government will crack down on the diamond business, as it has with coins. But for the moment, diamonds are one of the best ways to transfer wealth out of the country.

BRING MONEY HOME

Outside of actually travelling to a haven and bringing back under $10,000 in cash or diamonds, there exists a convenient but little known way of privately repatriating small amounts of money.

This repatriation of funds can be accomplished with utmost privacy by using a credit card where payment is automatically debited to one's Swiss bank account. All major cards are available--Visa, American Express and Diners Club. However, for the purposes of those reading this book, the Eurocard is probably best. The Eurocard is really three cards in one, depending on where one uses it. It is a Eurocard in Europe, an Access card in the U.K., and a Master-Card everywhere else.

The Eurocard Switzerland was developed by a pool of Swiss banks. It is offered by banks as a service to their clients. All information is therefore protected by banking secrecy laws. No third part is allowed access either to one's credit rating or purchase records at the Eurocard Switzerland office.

Properly used, this card can be a convenient and discreet way to withdraw small amounts of money. It is certainly much more private than having a bank mail one a check, as most checks are clearly marked with the bank's name and location and are usually payable through a large U.S. bank. One's affairs could, in this way, become an open book.

The Eurocard offers other conveniences in addition to privacy. For instance, travelers to Britain and Europe have found that certain stores and restaurants take Access or Eurocard but don't take American Express. In addition, having the card charges sent directly to one's bank means that there is no need to worry about writing a monthly check or making a payment deadline. Thus, if one were traveling or the bill became lost in the mail, otherwise substantial finance charges could be avoided.

The fact is that, used in Britain or Europe, charges do not clear through the U.S., so one's privacy is less likely to be invaded. However, this doesn't mean one can't use the card in the U.S. One simply has to make certain that, when using it, no more information about oneself is divulged than the name and number already on the card. For example, most stores and restaurants don't require an address or phone number when one is making a change. On the other hand, when checking into a hotel, one is usually asked for at least an address and sometimes even more personal information. The same is true for rental car transactions. One must, therefore, be discrete when using the card in certain situations.

In stores that take Master Card, the original sales slips are sent to the U.S. office, where they are kept. The U.S. office then informs the main Eurocard office in Brussels by telex, which, in turn, notifies Eurocard Switzerland in Zurich of the amount charged. The Zurich office notifies the specific bank, which debits the necessary amount from the account.

One can get a Eurocard by asking any bank for an application.

For each credit card that a bank issues a customer, that individual is required to put Sfr. 20,000 (approx. $10,000) into a blocked account in cash or equivalent assets. If held in cash, this account continues to draw interest. The client cannot, however, use these funds as long as he still possesses the charge card. Regardless of the country in which the original charge is made, Eurocard Switzerland bills the bank in Swiss francs. It is therefore most convenient for the client to maintain his charge account in Swiss francs. If he holds it in U.S. dollars or gold, these assets must be converted into francs to pay the bills.

If the client only has cash or assets totalling Sfr. 20,000 on account and still wants a charge card, he must replenish the account if changes totalling, say, Sfr. 5,000 are rung up. There is no hard and fast rule on the precise amount, but obviously, the more cash or assets to cushion the blocked account, the better for everyone.

If one holds other assets with the bank and card charges exceed Sfr. 20,000, one may choose to convert some of these assets to cover the account. Alternatively, one can either deposit more money or ask the bank for a loan. If the cardholder selects the latter, he can also choose the currency in which the loan will be denominated. Furthermore, the interest rate charged on the loan will be much less than that on Master Card or Visa in the United States, where the charge card interest rate is typically 19 - 20% on U.S. dollar balances. The U.S. dollar loan interest rates at most Swiss banks follow the money markets much more closely, being adjusted every month as conditions warrant. Currently (May 1986), the rate charged on U.S. dollar loans is a 8 1/2% plus 1/4% for each calendar quarter of unpaid balance. In other words, if one waits 2 1/2 months to repay the bank, one pays only an 8 1/2%

annual rate. Wait one year and the fee is 9 1/2%. If one keeps balances in Swiss francs and receives a bank loan denominated in this currency, the interest rate one pays will be even less. Current franc interest rates are 6% plus 1/4% per quarter.

These fees can change, but are still significantly lower than U.S. rates. This is another reason to consider using a charge card.

Incidentally, as of yet, Austrian banks offer credit card bills denominated only in Austrian Schillings. This makes the use of such a card cumbersome if one doesn't have a large schilling account. In fact, most European depositors in Austria have accounts denominated in either dollars or Swiss francs.

ONCE ABROAD

The question of what to do with one's funds once they are in a foreign bank is really only limited by one's imagination. Every major currency, every stock or bond in every major exchange, every major mutual fund or unit trust, in-house money management, all precious metals, insurance, all of these are available. To explore which of these investments is right for the individual at any point in time, or to what extent one's portfolio should be diversified internationally, would certainly require another book.

Chapter 10

References

CASSETTE TAPES

Offshore Diversification and Swiss Banking

Over two hours of narrative and interviews on such vital topics as choosing an offshore base, financial planning through international diversification, and offshore storage of bullion and numismatic coins. In addition, the cassettes take a detailed look at the practical side of using Swiss bank services. The cassette series was written and narrated by Harry Browne (available in October, 1986).

(MSI Inc., P.O. Box 91515, West Vancouver, B.C. Canada V7V 3P2/ US$ 39.95, postpaid)

CATALOGS

Eden Press Privacy Catalog

This unusual catalog is probably the most comprehensive list of books and special reports on privacy and closely related topics for the layman. Almost everyone will find at least one title worth buying.

(Eden Press, P.O. Box 8410, Fountain Valley, CA 92728
(714) 556-2023 or toll free in California (800) 338-8484.

International Services

This company offers a whole range of books and special reports by noted international strategist Gary A. Scott. His publications cover such topics as a world mutual fund survey and foreign currency borrowing/trading strategies. Scott also produces a monthly worldwide mutual fund rating service, Fund Help International.

(International Services, 3080 Tamiami Trail N., Suite 4A, Naples, FL 33940 (813) 261-1222.

Laissez-Faire Books

An excellent source for investment, privacy and tax strategy titles. This distributor has a wide following among investors and financial journalists.

(Laissez-Faire Books, 532 Broadway, 7th Floor, New York, NY 10012 (800) 238-2200.

Practicing Law Institute (PLI)

For the serious student of privacy law, international tax and financial planning matters this is the best source of titles. Although the PLI deals primarily with attorneys and CPAs the materials can be purchased by anyone. PLI publishes more than 400 specialized law books, loose leaf texts, and audio and video cassette programs. Many are transcripts of PLI seminars.

(Practicing Law Institute, 810 Seventh Avenue, New York, NY 10019 (212) 765-5700.

COIN STORAGE

<u>Complete Guide to Safe Storage of Silver and Gold</u>

Considered the definitive reference on this topic. The author, Christopher Weber, has done more formal research in this area than anyone else.

(DRA Publishing Co., 251 LaFayette Circle, LaFayette, CA 95494/ $68.00)

<u>National Association of Private Security Vaults</u>

This organization offers an accreditation program for members and has a referral service for the public.

(NAPSV), 135 West Morehead Street, Charlotte, North Carolina 28202/ (704) 372-7233)

CONSULTANTS

<u>Multicapital Services Inc.</u>

This firm assists investors in dealing with a whole range of activities necessary to obtain proper offshore diversification. This Swiss corporation has a North American office which makes it particularly convenient for Americans using their services.

(Multicapital Services, Inc., P.O. Box 91515, West Vancouver, B.C. Canada V7V 3P2 (604) 926-5811).

GEMSTONES

The Marcum Group

A full service organization offering gemstone and diamond brokerage, appraisals and independent, third party opinions on acquisitions and sales. The president, David Marcum, authored the Dow-Jones Irwin Guide to Fine Gems and Jewelry ($25.00) and publishes a monthly newsletter The Marcum Report ($89.00 for 12 issues) which is considered one of the most reliable sources of current price information and trends in the field.

(The Marcum Group, P.O. Box 606, Geneva, IL 60134 (312) 232-1583, Note: Both the book and newsletter can be ordered from this address. Also, the book is available in many bookstores.)

MAGAZINES

Resident Abroad

A superb monthly magazine that covers the world in search of new investment, privacy and lifestyle opportunities. The publication frequently carries a comprehensive list and current performance record for offshore unit trusts, insurance programs and individual managed accounts, many of which are not reported on by the U.S. and Canadian financial press due to regulatory barriers. Frequent articles on the basics of various types of investments are an added bonus.

(Resident Abroad, Marketing Department, Greystoke Place, Fetter Lane, London EC4A 1ND, England L56.00 or US$85.00 for airmail subscription for 12 issues.)

NEWSLETTERS

Harry Browne's Special Reports

A complete investment advisory service that places considerable emphasis on privacy and Swiss banking. Each issue comes as a pre-punched report for permanent filing in a custom three-ring binder provided with each subscription.

(Harry Browne Special Reports, Inc., P.O. Box 5586, Austin, Texas 78763 One ten-issue term $225.00).

International Living

A fascinating, easy-to-read newsletter that alerts subscribers to all manners of offshore opportunities from new retirement havens to real estate investment plays.

(International Living, 824 E. Baltimore, Street, MD 21202 $45.00 for 12 issues.)

Mark Skousen's Forecasts & Strategies

This monthly newsletter is almost universally regarded as the best ongoing source of information on practical financial privacy matters and new regulations. Every issue features a "Privacy Corner" column. The newsletter is also known for its down-to-earth investment advice. Request information on Skousen's special report "Secrets of Creating Private Tax-Free Wealth."

(Forecasts & Strategies, Phillips Publishing, Inc., 7811 Montrose Road, Potomac, MD 20854 (301) 424-3700 $135.00 for 12 issues).

Swiss Economic Viewpoint

This free, quarterly newsletter published by the Foreign Commerce Bank in Zurich, Switzerland, covers a wide range of topics, including privacy and using Swiss banking services for maximum efficiency.

(Swiss Economic Viewpoint, c/o Foreign Commerce Bank, P.O. Box 5022, 8022 Zurich, Switzerland).

SWISS BANKS REFERENCES

Harry Browne's Complete Guide to Swiss Banks

The classic book on Swiss banks. Although now almost ten years old it is still worth reading. According to Harry Browne, a second edition is now in preparation. For further information on either edition, write to Harry Browne's Special Reports.

(Harry Browne's Special Reports, Inc., P.O. Box 5586, Austin, Texas, 78763).

SWISS BANKS

Listed below are three Swiss banks that have reputations for efficient dealings with English-speaking clients.

Cambio + Valorenbank

P.O. Box 535
8021 Zurich
Switzerland

Telephone: 47-5400

(Street address: Utoquai 55, Zurich)

Foreign Commerce Bank (Representative Office)

P.O. Box 91491
West Vancouver, B.C.
Canada V7V 3P2
Telephone: (604) 925-3551

(Street address: 585 16th Street, West Vancouver, B.C., V7V 4S2)

or

Foreign Commerce Bank
P.O. Box 5022
8022 Zurich
Switzerland
Telephone: 482-6682

Ueberseebank, A.G.

Limmatquai 2-K
8024 Zurich
Switzerland
Telephone: 252-0304